ESSENT[

ORLANDO

★ Best places to see 34–55

■ Featured sight

Orlando 75–112

■ Around Orlando 113–148

■ Walt Disney World® Resort 149–185

Original text by Emma Stanford
Updated by Donna Dailey

© Automobile Association Developments Limited 2008
First published 2008

ISBN 978-0-7495-5367-8

Published by AA Publishing, a trading name of Automobile Association Developments Limited, whose registered office is Fanum House, Basing View, Basingstoke, Hampshire RG21 4EA.
Registered number 1878835.

Automobile Association Developments Limited retains the copyright in the original edition © 1998 and in all subsequent editions, reprints and amendments

A CIP catalogue record for this book is available from the British Library

All rights reserved. No part of this publication may be reproduced, stored in a retrieval system, or transmitted in any form or by any means – electronic, photocopying, recording or otherwise – unless the written permission of the publishers has been obtained beforehand. This book may not be sold, resold, hired out or otherwise disposed of by way of trade in any form of binding or cover other than that in which it is published, without the prior consent of the publisher. The contents of this publication are believed correct at the time of printing. Nevertheless, AA Publishing accept no responsibility for errors, omissions or changes in the details given, or for the consequences of readers' reliance on this information. This does not affect your statutory rights. Assessments of attractions, hotels and restaurants are based upon the author's own experience and contain subjective opinions that may not reflect the publisher's opinion or a reader's experience. We have tried to ensure accuracy, but things do change, so please let us know if you have any comments or corrections.

Colour separation: MRM Graphics Ltd
Printed and bound in Italy by Printer Trento S.r.l.

A03164
Maps in this title produced from
Map data © Global Mapping 2007
Transport map © Communicarta Ltd, UK

About this book

Symbols are used to denote the following categories:

- ✚ map reference to maps on cover
- ✉ address or location
- ☎ telephone number
- ⊙ opening times
- ✋ admission charge
- 🍴 restaurant or café on premises or nearby
- Ⓜ nearest underground train station
- 🚌 nearest bus/tram route
- 🚆 nearest overground train station
- ⛴ nearest ferry stop
- ✈ nearest airport
- ❓ other practical information
- ℹ tourist information office
- ▶ indicates the page where you will find a fuller description

This book is divided into six sections.

The essence of Orlando pages 6–19
Introduction; Features; Food and drink; Short break

Planning pages 20–33
Before you go; Getting there; Getting around; Being there

Best places to see pages 34–55
The unmissable highlights of any visit to Orlando

Best things to do pages 56–71
Great dinner shows; Free attractions; Spectator sports, Top golf courses and more

Exploring pages 72–185
The best places to visit in Orlando, organized by area

♦ to ♦♦♦♦♦ denotes AAA rating

Maps

All map references are to the maps on the covers. For example, Discovery Cove has the reference ✚ 8D – indicating the grid square in which it is to be found

Admission prices

Inexpensive (under $7);
Moderate ($8–$15);
Expensive ($15–$30);
Very expensive (over $30)

Hotel prices

Price are per room per night: **$** budget (under $100); **$$** moderate ($100–$200); **$$$** expensive to luxury (over $200)

Restaurant prices

Price for a three-course meal per person without drinks: **$** budget (under $18); **$$** moderate ($18–$32); **$$$** expensive (over $32)

Contents

THE ESSENCE OF... 6 – 19

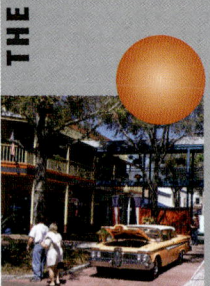

PLANNING 20 – 33

BEST PLACES TO SEE 34 – 55

BEST THINGS TO DO
56 – 71

EXPLORING...
72 – 185

The essence of...

Introduction	8–9
Features	10–11
Food and drink	12–15
Short break	16–19

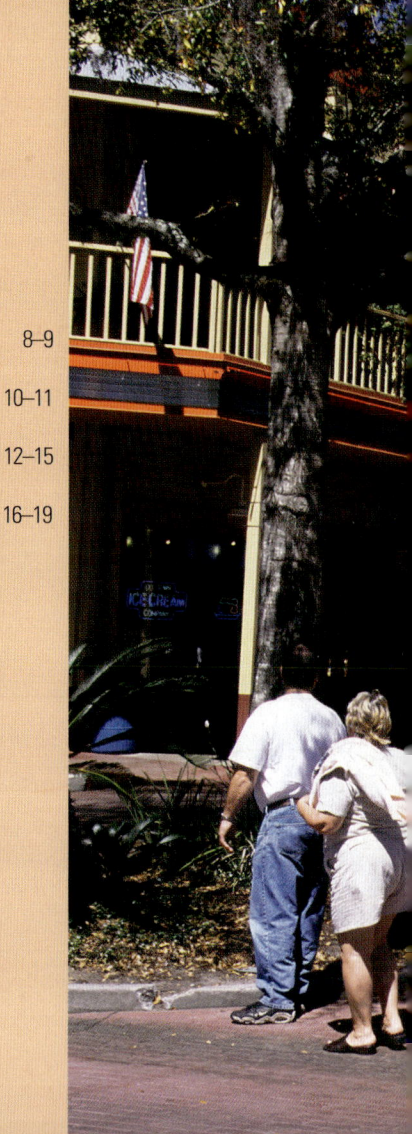

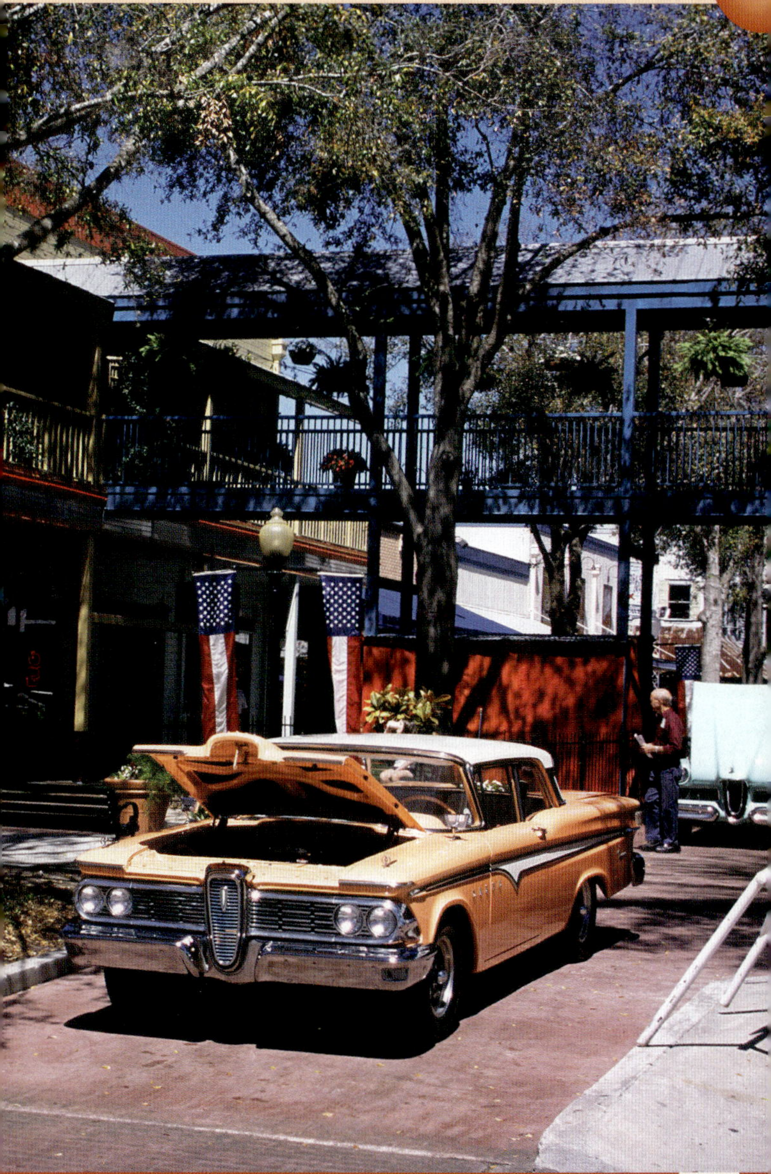

THE ESSENCE OF ORLANDO

THE ESSENCE OF ORLANDO

The essence of Orlando is entertainment. From the tips of Disney-MGM Studios' Earffel Tower down to the sandy bunkers of more than 170 golf courses, Orlando is a full-on, year-round crowd pleaser. Visitors can share their breakfast muffins with Goofy and the gang, get whisked aboard a Magic Carpet at the Arabian Nights dinner theater and never really set foot in Florida. But this would be a mistake. Beyond the man-made wonders, Central Florida offers sparkling lakes, citrus groves, lovely gardens and a rich and varied wildlife showcased in relaxing state parks.

THE ESSENCE OF ORLANDO

features

Orlando really is the town that Mickey Mouse built. A former cattle ranchers' watering hole and citrus depot in dusty Central Florida, the quiet country town boomed after the opening of the first Walt Disney World® theme park, Magic Kingdom®, in 1971. Today, Orlando is firmly established as one of the world's top vacation destinations.

About 50 million visitors pour into Orlando every year; over the past quarter century, over 500 million have visited Walt Disney World® Resort. The sheer volume of interest in Orlando has meant that the city has grown fast – often too fast for developers to concern themselves with the niceties of landscaping or public transportation – and the main tourist areas have spread out well beyond Orlando itself. Many visitors to Walt Disney World® Resort, a 30-minute drive south of heavily touristed International Drive, choose to stay in the neighboring town of Kissimmee. However, what Orlando may lack in aesthetic urban planning it more than makes up for in thrills and Disney magic. This is theme park heaven, boasting state-of-the-art rides, family entertainment and fantasy on tap. Add high standards of service and you have a vacation destination that could teach the rest of the world a thing or two.

10

THE ESSENCE OF ORLANDO

DISTANCES
- Distance from Miami: 236 miles (381km)
- Distance from New York: 944 miles (1,522km)
- Distance from Los Angeles: 2,203 miles (3,553km)
- Distance from London: 4,336 miles (6,994km)

SIZE
- Population: 213,200 (City of Orlando); 1.9 million (Greater Orlando)
- Population density: 2,200 people per square mile
- Annual visitors: 50 million

GEOGRAPHY
- Latitude: N 28° 32'
- Longitude: W 81° 22'
- Height above sea level: 70ft (21m)

FACILITIES
- Hotel rooms: 115,200
- Restaurants: 5,300-plus
- Visitor attractions: approximately 100
- Golf courses: 176-plus
- Water sports: 2,000-plus inland lakes, springs and rivers for fishing, swimming and boating; an hour's drive from the Atlantic and Gulf coasts
- Spectator sports: basketball (Orlando Magic and Women's NBA team, Orlando Miracle); baseball (Orlando Rays and spring training visitors, the Atlanta Braves and Houston Astros); American football (Orlando Predators)
- Retail shopping space: 52 million sq ft (4.6 million sq m)
- Transport: Orlando International Airport is the 12th busiest in the US (21st in the world), with hundreds of flights daily serving nearly 100 cities worldwide.

THE ESSENCE OF ORLANDO

food & drink

Orlando knows a bit about mass catering. From sunrise to sunset and long into the night, the city's 5,300-plus restaurants, cafeterias, family diners and take-away operations aim to satisfy the hunger of a wildly divergent public, and on the whole they do pretty well.

FLORIDA SPECIALTIES

Florida's two main food groups are commonly known as "surf 'n' turf" – that's seafood and beef. There are dozens of seafood restaurants in Orlando serving fresh fish, crab, lobster, shrimp and other delicacies. Steak houses and barbecue restaurants also do a roaring trade, and there is plenty of Southern-style Cajun or Creole influence in dishes, such as tasty blackened chicken or fish coated in spices and cooked over the grill.

BREAKFAST

For most visitors planning a long, busy day out and about sightseeing, the day begins with a traditional American breakfast, selected from a menu as long

THE ESSENCE OF ORLANDO

as your arm. Stockpile energy in the form of cereals, hot waffles or pancakes served with maple syrup, bacon, eggs and hash browns, sweet fruit or bran muffins, toast or plain "English muffins." In general, hotel buffet breakfasts are reasonably priced, and several motels and suite hotels include a basic breakfast of cereal, muffins and pastries with coffee and fruit juice in the room price.

THE ESSENCE OF ORLANDO

LUNCH
Lunch on the sightseeing trail often means alarming lines in the theme parks. The busiest time is between 12 and 2, so if you can manage to eat earlier or later it does make things easier. Guests who prefer a sit-down meal in a service restaurant at lunchtime should make reservations at the Guest Relations window when they arrive at the park. Otherwise there is usually a wide choice of eateries, from self-service cafeterias to hot dog stands, barbecue take-aways, sandwiches, burgers and ice creams, which can be eaten at outdoor seating areas.

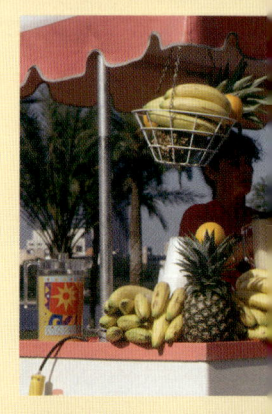

DINNER
The evening meal is a very flexible affair in Orlando. Some restaurants start serving at 4pm to cater for those who have missed out on lunch or determined budget eaters who make the best of "early bird specials," discounted meals offered before the restaurants really begin to fill up at around 6:30–7.

The main non-Walt Disney World® Resort areas – International Drive and Kissimmee – are well provided with inexpensive family restaurants and fast food chains, as well as medium-price range steak houses, American, Chinese, Italian and Mexican eateries. For something more up-market,

THE ESSENCE OF ORLANDO

look to the top hotels, such as the Peabody Orlando, for a chance to dress up and enjoy a gourmet meal in notably elegant surroundings.

Medium-price bracket and expensive hotels generally provide a choice of dining options, and this is certainly true of the Walt Disney World® Resort complexes. Restaurants serving up a selection of walking, talking oversized Disney characters along with their menu are a favorite with children, but do remember to reserve ahead to avoid disappointment.

DRINKING

Sightseeing is thirsty work in Orlando, and several rounds of soft drinks for the whole family at theme park or hotel prices can prove an expensive business. If you are on a budget, it is a good idea to stock up on bottled water, fruit juices or multi-packs of canned soft drinks at a supermarket. To buy or consume alcohol legally in the state of Florida, customers must be 21 or over.

THE ESSENCE OF ORLANDO

short break

If you only have a short time to visit Orlando, or would like to get a really complete picture of the region, here are the essentials:

- **Blooming marvellous:** for local horticultural color, enjoy the formal delights of the Harry P. Leu Gardens (➤ 42–43), or the woodland trails of the Historic Bok Sanctuary (➤ 127).

- **Shop 'til you drop:** the top end of Orlando's International Drive has turned into a magnet for bargain-hunters, with factory outlet stores galore.

- **Do the birdwalk,** a little-known secret: the Gatorland marsh boardwalk is one of the best birdwatching spots in the region (➤ 76–77).

THE ESSENCE OF ORLANDO

- **Silver Spurs:** cattle ranchers first settled the area in the 1840s and Kissimmee celebrates its origins with the biannual Silver Spurs Rodeo (➤ 129).

- **Manatees,** or sea cows, are the endangered gentle giants of Florida's waterways. If you can't get to see them in the wild (➤ 120–121), do not miss SeaWorld's Manatees: The Last Generation? (➤ 46–47).

17

THE ESSENCE OF ORLANDO

● **Make a splash!** When the heat and humidity get too much take a break from the theme parks and cool off at any of the water parks in Orlando (➤ 60).

© Disney

THE ESSENCE OF ORLANDO

- **Drink up!** Florida produces around 75 percent of the nation's citrus crop, so be sure to sample fresh local juices.

- **Amazing Adventures of Spider-Man**®: Universal's Islands of Adventure®'s incredible blend of indoor fireworks, villains, virtual reality and unbelievably surreal sensations makes this a must-see.

- **Magic Kingdom**®: the "must see" Disney park (➤ 168–173).

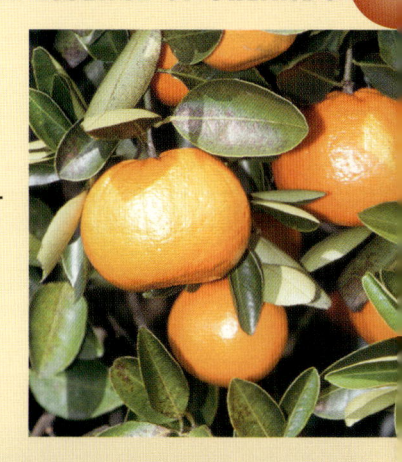

- **Doing dinner** can be quite an event in Orlando. A host of popular dinner theaters offers themed evenings from Medieval Times to 1930s-style Capone's (➤ 64–65).

Planning

Before you go	22–25
Getting there	26–27
Getting around	28–29
Being there	30–33

21

PLANNING

Before you go

WHEN TO GO

JAN	FEB	MAR	APR	MAY	JUN	JUL	AUG	SEP	OCT	NOV	DEC
22°C	23°C	25°C	27°C	27°C	30°C	32°C	32°C	30°C	28°C	25°C	22°C
72°F	73°F	77°F	81°F	81°F	86°F	90°F	90°F	86°F	82°F	77°F	72°F

● High season ● Low season

The warmest months in Orlando are July–August with temperatures reaching highs of 92°F (33°C) and lows of 73°F (23°C). Even in the coolest month of January temperatures can still reach 72°F (22°C) but they can also dip to as low as 49°F (9°C).

Summer storms in July normally see this month being the wettest as well as the hottest with up to 7.8in (20cm) of rain falling in contrast to only 1.8in (5cm) from November to December. In these sticky summer months the mornings are often fine and dry, with thunderstorms more common in the afternoon – in most cases you can queue under cover but it is wise to pack waterproofs or buy a waterproof poncho from one of the many merchandise carts at the parks.

The chart figures above are the average daily maximum for each month.

WHAT YOU NEED

- ● Required
- ○ Suggested
- ▲ Not required

Some countries require a passport to remain valid for a minimum period (usually at least six months) beyond the date of entry.

	UK	Germany	USA	Netherlands	Spain
Passport/ National Identity Card	●	●	▲	●	●
Visa (Waiver form to be completed)	▲	▲	▲	▲	▲
Onward or Return Ticket	●	●	▲	●	●
Health Inoculations (tetanus)	○	○	○	○	○
Health Documentation (▶ 23, Health insurance)	▲	▲	▲	▲	▲
Travel Insurance	●	●	▲	●	●
Driving Licence (national or International Driving Permit)	●	●	●	●	●
Car Insurance Certificate	○	○	●	○	○
Car Registration Document	●	●	●	●	●

BEFORE YOU GO

WEBSITES
Further details on attractions, dining, shopping, nightlife and recreation are available from:

www.orlandoinfo.com/uk
www.floridakiss.com
www.floridastateparks.org
www.floridatraveluse.com

TOURIST OFFICES AT HOME
In the UK
Orlando/Kissimmee–St. Cloud Tourism Bureau, Inc. Visitor information and a free Orlando/Kissimmee pack of visitor guides to both areas and local map ☎ 020 7233 2305 or 0800 092 2352 (brochure line)

Visit Florida
For an *Official Florida Holiday Guide* ☎ 01737 644882 in the UK. Visit Florida also provide a free phone tourist assistance hotline in Florida ☎ 1-800 656 8777 or 888/735-2872. Further information from www.visitflorida.com

HEALTH INSURANCE
Medical insurance cover of at least $1,000,000 unlimited cover is strongly recommended, as medical bills can be astronomical and treatment may be withheld if you have no evidence of means to pay. Your medical insurance cover should include dental treatment, which is readily available, but expensive. Have a check up before you go. Dental referral telephone numbers are in the Yellow Pages telephone directory or ask at the desk of your hotel.

TIME DIFFERENCES

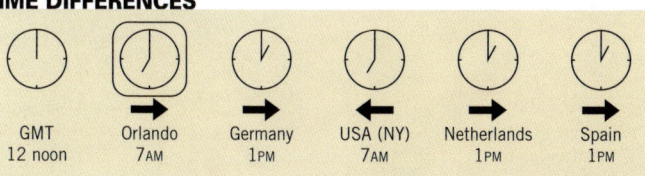

GMT	Orlando	Germany	USA (NY)	Netherlands	Spain
12 noon	7AM	1PM	7AM	1PM	1PM

Orlando local time is Eastern Standard Time (the same as New York) which is five hours behind Greenwich Mean Time (GMT–5). Daylight saving applies, with clocks one hour ahead between March and October.

PLANNING

NATIONAL HOLIDAYS

Jan 1 *New Year's Day*
Jan (third Mon) *Martin Luther King Day*
Feb (third Mon) *Presidents' Day*
Mar/Apr *Good Friday*
May (last Mon) *Memorial Day*
Jul 4 *Independence Day*
Sep (first Mon) *Labor Day*
Oct (second Mon) *Columbus Day*
Nov 11 *Veterans' Day*
Nov (fourth Thu) *Thanksgiving*
Dec 25 *Christmas Day*
Boxing Day is not a public holiday in the US. Some shops open on National Holidays.

WHAT'S ON WHEN

January *Capital One Bowl:* Nationally televised college football game on New Year's Day.
February *Festival of Rhythm & Blues:* Celebrates Black History Month at Kissimmee Lakefront Park.
Silver Spurs Rodeo: Major event on the Professional Rodeo Cowboys Association circuit held in Kissimmee.
Daytona 500: NASCAR race held at Daytona International Speedway.
March *Florida Strawberry Festival:* Held in Plant City (between Orlando and Tampa), this is a hugely popular event with country music, agricultural shows and fair rides.

BEFORE YOU GO

Kissimmee Bluegrass Festival: Week-long toe-tapping music event.
Winter Park Sidewalk Arts Festival: long weekend of art, food, music and activities.
April *Central Florida Fair:* Equestrian shows, foot-stomping music and a carnival midway with rides and games at the Central Florida Fairgrounds.
Epcot International Flower & Garden Festival: garden and greenhouse tours, demonstrations and displays.
Kissimmee Jazz Fest: Top jazz artists, local musicians, crafts and food at Lakefront Park.
May *Florida Music Festival:* Three-day event with up-and-coming musicians, one of the best in the Southeast, held in downtown Orlando.
Zellwood Sweet Corn Festival: 200,000 corn on the cobs get consumed over the weekend at this family event.
June *Fiesta San Juan:* Annual celebration of Latin culture with food, music and dancing at Wet 'n Wild.
July *Lake Eola Fireworks over the Fountain:* Orlando celebrates the Fourth of July with games, activities and fireworks in Lake Eola Park.
September *Caribbean Festival and Italian Festival:* Themed weekends at Silver Springs with music, dancing, specialty dishes and festivities.
October *Walt Disney World® Golf Classic:* Top golfers gather for this annual PGA Tour event, played on the Palm and Magnolia courses.
Silver Spurs Rodeo: the cowboys are back in Kissimmee.
November *Cypress Gardens Mum (Chrysanthemum) Festival:* 3 million blooms in spectacular displays.
Annual Festival of the Masters: Art show at Downtown Disney®.
Fall Fiesta in the Park: Two-day arts and crafts show with 600 artisans, food and live entertainment in downtown Orlando's Lake Eola Park.
Festival of Lights at Silver Springs: Over 1 million twinkle lights, neon displays, choirs and a lighted boat parade, weekends late November–December.
December *Cypress Gardens Poinsettia Festival & Garden of Lights:* 400,000 lights and 40,000 poinsettias for Christmas.
Mickey's Very Merry Christmas Party: Celebrations at Magic Kingdom®.
Holiday Extravaganza: Strolling performers, live entertainment, spectacular fireworks and 20 tons of snow at Kissimmee Lakefront Park.
Orlando Citrus Parade: Marching bands and citrus floats made from thousands of pieces of grapefruit, oranges and tangerines.

PLANNING

Getting there

BY AIR

Orlando International Airport

9 miles to city center

- 🚆 N/A
- 🚌 45 minutes
- 🚗 30 minutes

Tampa International Airport

85 miles to city center

- 🚆 2 hours
- 🚌 2 hours
- 🚗 90 minutes

BY AIR

Orlando is a major domestic and an international airport. There are non-stop flights from about 70 different US destinations, and links to more than 100 cities worldwide. It is easily accessible and within 15 miles (24km) of major attractions, such as Walt Disney World® Resort, and downtown Orlando. Airport ☎ 407/825-2355.

The nearest alternative international gateway for scheduled flights is Tampa, 1½ hours from Orlando; several charter operators serve Orlando Sanford, 20 minutes away.

BY RAIL

Amtrak trains serve Orlando with four daily trains originating in New York, and Miami, also stopping at Winter Park and Sanford, north of the city, and Kissimmee near Walt Disney World® Resort. Amtrak offers an Auto Train overnight service with sleepers, which conveys passengers with their vehicles and runs daily between Lorton, Va and Sanford, Florida. For general information ☎ 1-800 872 7245 (toll free).

BY CAR

Interstate 4, or I-4, the area's main interstate highway, passes through Orlando and connects it with other parts of Florida. It runs roughly parallel to International Drive where many of the main attractions, hotels,

GETTING THERE

restaurants and shops are located. US 192, also known as the Irlo Bronson Memorial Highway, intersects with I-4 and leads to Walt Disney World® Resort and many Kissimmee hotels.

BY BUS

Greyhound lines serve Orlando from many centers in the US: within the metropolitan area local buses provide a good service, notably Mears Transportation, which serves the airport and most of Orlando's main attractions and hotels. Greyhound bus ☎ 1-800 231 2222 (toll free); www.greyhound.com. For excursions around the area and to the major attractions, tour companies offer diverse itineraries or can customize trips for groups.

Getting around

PUBLIC TRANSPORT
Short-stay visitors can tackle Orlando without a car, though public transportation is pretty sketchy. Most hotels offer free shuttles to Walt Disney World® Resort, and Orlando's International Drive area has the inexpensive and efficient I-Ride trolley bus (8am–10:30pm) with scheduled stops every 20 minutes (see below).

Urban Transport Besides cab and limousine service to anywhere in the Greater Orlando area, the city's Lynx bus system provides economical public transportation around Orlando (☎ 407/841-8240, www.golynx.com). Bus stops are marked with a "paw" print of a Lynx cat.

The I-Ride Trolley serves International Drive, with stops every 20 minutes (☎ 407/354-5656; www.iridetrolley.com). The stops are marked "I-RIDE" at each Lynx bus stop. A second route, the Green Line trolley, serves the Major Boulevard business district, Universal Boulevard and South International Drive.

TAXIS
Cabs are plentiful in Orlando, but they are not accustomed to being hailed down in the street. Hotels are the best places to find a cab. If money is no object, limousine transportation can be easily arranged through your hotel's guest services desk.

DRIVING
- The Americans drive on the right side of the road.
- Seat belts must be worn by drivers and front-seat passengers. Children under four must use child safety seats; older children must use a safety seat or seat belt.
- Random breath-testing. Never drive under the influence of alcohol.

GETTING AROUND

- Gas or gasoline (petrol), is cheaper in America than in Europe. It is sold in American gallons (five American gallons equal 18L), and comes in three grades, all unleaded. Many gas stations have automatic vending machines that accept notes and major credit cards.
- Speed limits, which are strictly enforced, are as follows:
  Interstate highways: 55–70mph/88–112kph
  Main roads: 55mph/88kph
  Urban roads: 20–30mph/32–48kph
- If you break down pull over, raise the hood (bonnet), switch on the hazard lights, and call the rental company or the breakdown number, which should be displayed on or near the dashboard. For added security, several major rental car agencies (including Alamo, Avis and Hertz) are now offering clients the option to rent an in-car cell phone.

CAR RENTAL

Rates are very competitive. Take an unlimited mileage deal, collision damage waiver and adequate (more than minimal) insurance. There is a surcharge on drivers under 25 and the minimum age is often 21 (sometimes 25). Expect to pay by credit card.

CONCESSIONS

Students with student ID cards and seniors age 55 and above can usually receive discounts on admission to museums and attractions. Most have reduced children's tickets (ages vary, but usually age 3–9) and free admission for children under 3.

Orlando's free Preferred Visitor Magicard gives discounts on attractions, accommodations, dining and transport. More information is available on www.orlandoinfo.com or from the tourist office

The theme parks have a host of multi-day and multi-park ticket options, so be sure and study them carefully and compare prices. You can sometimes (but not always) save money by booking online or in advance – at Universal Orlando tickets are cheapest by phone. Options include Disney's 7-day Magic Your Way base ticket, and Orlando Flex Tickets, which include unlimited admission for 14 consecutive days, available from participating parks. Four-park Flex tickets cover Universal Studios®, Islands of Adventure®, SeaWorld and Wet 'n Wild, five-park tickets also include Busch Gardens.

PLANNING

Being there

TOURIST OFFICES
Official Visitor Center
8723 International Drive, Gala Center (cnr Austrian Row)
Orlando, Florida 32819
☎ 407/363-5872;
www.orlandoinfo.com
🕐 All year 8–7

Daytona Beach Area Convention and Visitors Center
Visitor Information Center, Daytona USA, 1801 W International Speedway Boulevard
☎ 386/253-8669 or 1-800 854 1234 or 1-866 644 9648
🕐 Daily 9–7

Florida's Space Coast Office of Tourism
8810 Astronaut Boulevard, Cape Canaveral
☎ 321/637-5483 or 1-800 936 2326
Information desks at Kennedy Space Center Visitor Complex; www.space-coast.com

Kissimmee – St. Cloud Convention and Visitors Bureau
Visitor Information Center, 1925 E Irlo Bronson Memorial Highway/US192
☎ 407/847-5000 or 1-800 333 KISS (5477); www.floridakiss.com
🕐 Mon–Fri 8–5

Tampa Bay Visitor Information Center
615 Channelside Drive
☎ 813/223-2752;
www.visittampabay.com
🕐 Daily 9:30–5

MONEY
The US dollar ($) is the official currency in the United States. Dollar bills come in 1, 5, 10, 20, 50, 100 and 500 denominations. Note that all dollar bills are the same size and color – all greenbacks. One dollar is made up of 100 cents. Coins are of 1 cent (pennies), 5 cents (nickel), 10 cents (dime), 25 cents (quarter) and 1 dollar.

An unlimited amount of US dollars can be imported or exported, but amounts of over $10,000 must be reported to US Customs, as should similar amounts of gold. US dollars traveler's checks are accepted as cash in most places (not cabs) as are major credit cards.

BEING THERE

TIPS/GRATUITIES

Yes ✓   No ✗
It is useful to have plenty of small notes

Hotels (chambermaid, doorman etc)	✓	$1
Restaurants (waiter, waitresses)	✓	15/20%
Bar Service	✓	15%
Cabs	✓	15%
Tour guides (discretionary)	✓	
Porters	✓	$1 per bag
Lavatories	✗	

POSTAL AND INTERNET SERVICES

Post offices in Orlando are few and far between. Stamps from vending machines are sold at a 25 percent premium; it is best to buy them at your hotel. The international postcard rate is 75 cents. Post offices are usually open Monday to Friday 9am–5pm, but many hotels and major attractions provide a post office service out of hours.

Internet access is available at internet cafés, hotel rooms and business centers, and other locations such as Kinko's copying centers. Prices vary but are generally inexpensive. Many hotels and cafés have free WiFi access.

TELEPHONES

There are telephones in hotel lobbies, drug stores, restaurants, garages and at the roadside. A local call costs 25–50 cents. Buy cards for long distance calls from the Official Visitors Center, some pharmacies and grocery stores. Dial "0" for the operator. "Collect" means reverse the charges. Toll-free numbers usually begin with 1-800, 1-877 or 1-866.

International dialling codes
From Orlando (US) to:
UK: 011 44
Ireland: 011 353
Australia: 011 61
Germany: 011 49
Netherlands: 011 31
Spain: 011 34

Emergency telephone numbers
Police 911
Fire 911
Ambulance 911
Police (non emergency):
☎ 407/246-2414

PLANNING

EMBASSIES AND CONSULATES
UK ☎ 407/254-3300
Germany ☎ 202/298-4320 (Washington)
Netherlands ☎ 786/866-0480
Spain ☎ 305/446-5511 (Miami)

HEALTH ADVICE
Sun advice
By far the most common source of ill health in Florida is too much sun. Orlando in summer is very hot and humid and the sun is strong all year round. Use a sunscreen, wear a hat outdoors and ensure that everyone drinks plenty of fluids.

Drugs
Medicines can be bought at drug stores, certain drugs generally available elsewhere require a prescription in the US. Acetaminophen is the US equivalent of paracetamol. Take an insect repellent including Deet and cover up after dark, to avoid being bitten by mosquitoes.

Safe water
Restaurants usually provide a jug of iced water. Drinking unboiled water from taps is safe but not always very pleasant. Mineral water is inexpensive and readily available.

PERSONAL SAFETY
Orlando is not generally a dangerous place but to help prevent crime and accidents:
- Never open your hotel room door unless you know who is there. If in doubt call hotel security.
- Place valuables in a safety deposit box.
- Always lock your front and/or patio doors when in the room and when leaving. Use the safety chain/lock for security.
- When driving, keep all car doors locked.
- Never approach alligators, they can outrun a man.

ELECTRICITY
The power supply is 110/120 volts AC (60 cycles). Electrical sockets take two-prong, flat-pin plugs. Visitors should bring adaptors for their 3-pin and 2-round-pin plugs.

BEING THERE

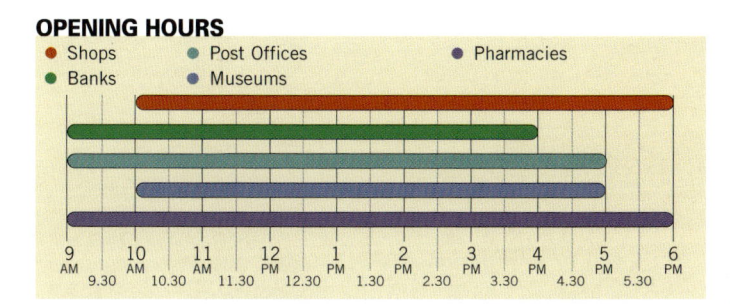

OPENING HOURS

- Shops
- Banks
- Post Offices
- Museums
- Pharmacies

Shops	10.30 AM – 6 PM		
Banks	9.30 AM – 4 PM		
Post Offices	9 AM – 5 PM		
Museums	10 AM – 5 PM		
Pharmacies	9 AM – 6 PM		

There are two all-night pharmacies: Ekered Drugs, 908 Lee Road, and Walgreen Drug Store, International Drive (opposite Wet 'n Wild). Some shops in malls and on International Drive open until 9pm. Post offices are few and far between; hotels are usually helpful with postal matters. Banks, offices and post offices close on Saturday. Opening times of theme parks vary with seasonal demand. Opening times of museums vary; check with individual museum, some are closed on a Monday.

LANGUAGE

The official language of the USA is English. Spanish is also widely spoken. Certain words have a different meaning in American English, below are a few examples of such words and their British English equivalent.

ground floor	*first floor*	second floor	*third floor*
first floor	*second floor*	lift	*elevator*
1 cent coin	*penny*	banknote	*bill*
5 cent coin	*nickel*	banknote (colloquial)	*greenback*
10 cent coin	*dime*	dollar (colloquial)	*buck*
25 cent coin	*quarter*	cashpoint	*automatic teller*
grilled	*broiled*	chips (potato)	*fries*
prawns	*shrimp*	crisps (potato)	*chips*
aubergine	*eggplant*	jam	*jelly*
courgette	*zucchini*	spirit	*liquor*
maize	*corn*	soft drink	*soda*

Best places to see

Busch Gardens	36–37
Cypress Gardens Adventure Park	38–39
Discovery Cove	40–41
Harry P Leu Gardens	42–43
Kennedy Space Center	44–45
SeaWorld Orlando	46–47
Silver Springs	48–49
Wet 'n Wild	50–51
Walt Disney World® Resort	52–53
Universal Orlando® Resort	54–55

© Disney

35

BEST PLACES TO SEE

1 Busch Gardens

www.buschgardens.com

The combination of exotic animals, thrilling roller-coasters, water rides and shows makes this one of Florida's top attractions.

Busch Gardens lies around 75 minutes' drive west of Orlando, in Tampa. Opened in 1959, it is a seasoned crowd-pleaser with pleasantly mature grounds shaded by trees and flowering shrubs. The overall plot is "Africa," with 10 themed areas such as Nairobi, Timbuktu and the Serengeti Plain; which incorporates the interactive Edge of Africa domain. It can be seen on the Serengeti Express Railway.

The 350-acre (141-ha) park houses one of the nation's premier zoos. There are more than 2,700 animals from over 300 species wandering the grassland enclosures of the Serengeti Plain, inhabiting the rocks and waterfalls of the Great Ape Domain and featured in other displays such as the Bird Gardens. Busch Gardens plays a significant role in breeding and conserving endangered species and many of the zoo's latest additions are proudly displayed in the Nairobi Animal Nursery.

But animals are by no means all the park has to offer: roller-coaster fans are also in for a big treat. Check out the duelling, double wooden roller-coaster Gwazi and Montu, one of the tallest and longest inverted coasters in the world. The Kumba ride remains among the largest and fastest steel

BEST PLACES TO SEE

roller-coasters in existence, and assorted water rides provide varying degrees of thrills and spills, plus a chance to cool off in the Florida sunshine.

Small children are particularly well catered-for here. In addition to the animal attractions, there is the interactive Land of the Dragons play area, and colorful "Lion King" style show in the Moroccan Palace Theater. Strollers are available for rental in the Morocco district and there is a full baby-changing and nursing area in Land of the Dragons.

See also ➤ 114–119.

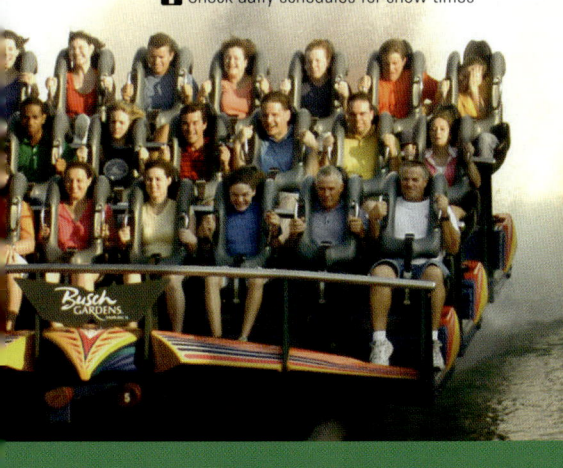

✚ *25b (off map)* ✉ Busch Boulevard, Tampa (75 miles/121km west of Orlando via I-4 West and I-75 North to Fowler Avenue/Exit 265) ☎ 813/987-5082 or 1-888 800 5447 ⏰ Daily 10–6 (extended summer and hols) ✋ Very expensive 🍴 Refreshment stops throughout park, plus the full-service Crown Colony Restaurant (Crown Colony) ($–$$) ❓ Check daily schedules for show times

BEST PLACES TO SEE

2 Cypress Gardens Adventure Park

www.cypressgardens.com

Florida's first theme park remains faithful to its botanical origins and is famous for its four annual flower festivals.

Sloping gently down to the shores of Lake Eloise, near Winter Haven, a 45-minute drive south of Orlando, Cypress Gardens was originally laid out in the 1930s along the swampy water's edge, shaded by giant cypress trees. The park has expanded considerably since, covering more than 220 acres (89ha), and offers a variety of shows, shopping, dining and animal attractions in addition to the

BEST PLACES TO SEE

carefully manicured gardens, eye-catching topiary and other horticultural exhibits.

For plant-lovers, the lush Botanical Gardens remain the highlight of a visit. Shaded brick paths meander through dense tropical plantings of heliconias and bromeliads, cascades of brilliantly colored bougainvillea and forests of bamboo.

But flower power aside, Cypress Gardens takes pride in its water-ski revues on the lake, and the 153-ft (47-m) high Island in the Sky revolving observatory. At its foot, Jubilee Junction houses snack stops, restaurants and shops.

Other attractions concentrate on the wonders of the natural world, with the Wings of Wonder Butterfly Conservatory and the Nature's Way area featuring animal enclosures and a wooden boardwalk area on the lake. A recent addition is a kid-pleasing assortment of amusement rides: tilt-a-whirls, roller coasters, flume rides, and other cars and cages that flip, spin and roll. To be sure, however, this is still a botanical garden at heart and a good place to experience an old-fashioned Florida attraction.

✠ *26a* ✉ SR540 West 4 miles (6.5km) east of Winter Haven, off US27, 22 miles (35km) south of I-4 ☎ 863/324-2111 ⓘ Daily 10–6 (closing times vary) 🍴 Aunt Julie's Country Kitchen ($–$$); Backwater Bill's BBQ ($); Sandra Dee's Diner ($); Village Fare Food Court ($); assorted snack and refreshment stops ($) ✋ Very expensive

BEST PLACES TO SEE

3 Discovery Cove

www.discoverycove.com

Swim with dolphins, rays and thousands of tropical fish then laze on the sand at this beach paradise created in landlocked Orlando.

To swim with dolphins is a cherished dream for millions, so it should come as no surprise that somebody in Orlando came up with the brilliant idea of creating a theme park where this particular dream can come true. Sister to the world-famous SeaWorld Orlando (➤ 46–47) theme park across the road (and Busch Gardens in Tampa, ➤ 36–37, 114–119). Unlike other theme parks, which rely on a high turnover of guests, Discovery Cove aims for exclusivity. Admission is by advance reservation only and limited to 1,000 guests per day ensuring the park is never over-run and the all-important dolphin-swim program is not compromised.

BEST PLACES TO SEE

As well as the 45-minute dolphin swim guests can snorkel among thousands of tropical reef fish from 90 different species in a coral reef setting, while sharks and barracudas patrol just a few inches away behind plexiglass safety panels. While at Ray Lagoon they can wade into a world of sleek and mysterious rays as dozens of southern and cownose stingrays, which can grow up to 4ft (1.25m) across, glide past to be touched and fed little snacks. For those looking to relax there is plenty of space on the sandy beaches around the resort-style swimming pool, or guests can take a gentle meander down Tropical River which flows past sunken ruins and hidden grottoes, waterfalls and beaches to the 12,000-sq ft (1,115-sq m) aviary. For an additional fee, you can also get behind the scenes. The park offers a Trainer for a Day program for just 12 guests a day where you can work side-by-side with animal experts.

A day at Discovery Cove may seem like a very expensive option (about $275), but keep in mind that everything is included from towel and snorkel to wetsuit, and you'll have a very nice lunch that enhances your day.

✛ 8D ✉ 6000 Discovery Cove Way (1-4/Exit 71 or 72) ☎ 407/370-1280 or 1-877 434 7268 🕐 Daily 8–5:30 ✋ Very expensive; a reduced package is available for children 3–5 and guests who do not take part in the dolphin swim 🍴 Breakfast and lunch in the Laguna Grill is included in the admission price; the Oasis snack cabanas ($) serve refreshments 🚌 I-Ride, Lynx #42 ❓ The hands-on Trainer for a Day program is available for up to 12 guests a day. Reservations essential

BEST PLACES TO SEE

4 Harry P Leu Gardens

www.leugardens.org

Three miles of walkways take you through a series of beautiful themed gardens created by Harry Leu and his wife.

Sloping down to the shores of Lake Rowena, these lovely 50-acre (20-ha) gardens provide a soothing escape from the hustle and bustle. They were originally laid out by local businessman Harry P Leu and his wife, who purchased the property in 1936 and lived in historic Leu House, a much-enlarged pioneer home that now houses a museum.

Near the entrance, the lush Ravine Garden leads down to a boardwalk and a gazebo which overlooks the lake. Coots and ducks potter about in the lake's waters and the occasional wild alligator lurks here. To the west of the property, mature southern magnolias and spreading live oaks shade the camellia woods, which can be seen at their best during the October to March flowering season. The Leus planted more than 2,000 camellia specimens here, and their collection is considered to be one of the finest in the eastern US.

The floral centerpiece is the Rose Garden, a popular setting for open-air weddings among the 1,000 scented rose bushes. Close by, Leu House is open for regular tours. In the far corner of the gardens, the Display Greenhouse is a riot of hothouse orchids, tropical gingers, anthuriums, heliconias and ferns.

✚ 22M   ✉ 1920 N Forest Avenue   ☎ 407/246-2620
🕐 Daily 9–5 except Christmas Day. Leu House tours daily 10–3:30 (last tour)   ✋ Inexpensive

BEST PLACES TO SEE

5 Kennedy Space Center

www.kennedyspacecenter.com

Tours, films, rockets and space hardware bring the American space program to life at NASA's Florida space launch facility.

The Kennedy Space Center Visitor Complex is the gateway to Launch Complex 39, where space shuttles will one day again blast off into orbit, and where *Apollo 11* set off on its ground-breaking journey to deliver the first man to walk on the moon in 1969. A visit to the Space Center offers a terrific opportunity to delve into the history of the US space program, experience a nail-biting re-creation of the countdown to blast off and get a behind-the-scenes view of past and future space technology.

The very first rockets launched from Cape Canaveral were long-range guided missiles fired from Cape Canaveral Air Force Station in the early 1950s. NASA, the National Aeronautics and Space Administration established in 1958 to carry out the peaceful exploration and use of space, later used the site to prepare and launch science satellites and the manned and unmanned flights of the early Mercury and Gemini programs. In 1964, NASA transferred operations to Launch Complex 39, at Merritt Island, which was designed to handle the Apollo-Saturn V program. The first launch from the

BEST PLACES TO SEE

Kennedy Space Center was the Apollo 8 mission December 1968.

Today, bus tours offer views of the shuttle launch pads, the gargantuan Vehicle Assembly Building (VAB) and make a stop at the spectacular $37-million Apollo/Saturn V Center, which features an actual, unused, *Saturn V* rocket. Families with small children will find a half-day visit long enough. But do save time to watch at least one IMAX movie (included in admission). "Magnificent Desolation: Walking on the Moon 3-D" and "Space Station 3-D" are inspiring.

✛ *32d* ✉ SR405, Merritt Island (Bee Line Expressway/SR528 toll road east from Orlando)
☎ 321/449-4444 or 321/454-4198 TDD 🕐 Daily 9–dusk
✋ Expensive 🍴 Mila's ($–$$); cafés and concessions ($)
❓ Bus tours depart regularly (allow 2.5 hours).

SeaWorld Orlando

www.seaworld.com

Shamu, the killer whale, star of SeaWorld, heads up an all-star cast at the world's most popular sea life park.

Laid out over an action-packed 200-acre (81-ha) site, SeaWorld provides a full day's itinerary of shows and marine encounters in the best theme park tradition. The stars of the shows are almost exclusively of the finned or flippered variety and their virtuoso performances (coaxed by the strategic deployment of fish) are a source of continuous amazement and delight to packed audiences. Though SeaWorld can get very busy, its built-in advantage over other traditional parks is the scarcity of rides, so there are few long lines.

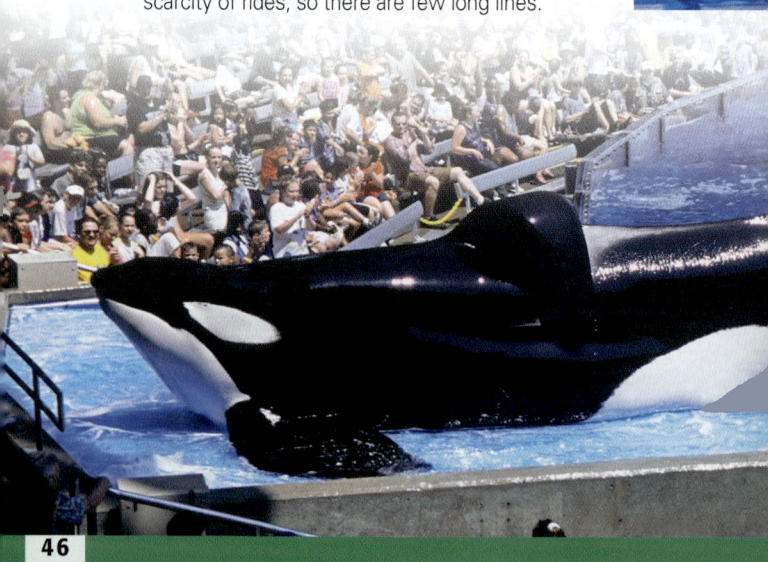

BEST PLACES TO SEE

Shamu shows, especially the evening version – Shamu Rocks America – are hugely popular and performances in the Whale & Dolphin Stadium and the Sea Lion & Otter Stadium are a must. The Penguin Encounter (with real snow) should not be missed, and anybody who has never seen a manatee should rectify this immediately at Manatees: The Last Generation?

SeaWorld pushes its role as a significant animal rescue, conservation and research facility. There are several entertaining and educational behind-the-scenes tours for interested guests as well as summer camp adventures. For an even more interactive experience, SeaWorld's sister park, Discovery Cove, invites guests to swim with bottlenose dolphins and tropical fish (➤ 40–41). See also ➤ 83–87.

🕂 8D ✉ 7007 SeaWorld Drive, Orlando (I-4/Exit 71 or 72 ☎ 407/351-3600 or 1-800 432 1178 🕒 Daily 9–7 (extended summer and hols) 👋 Very expensive. There is a 10 percent discount for ticket purchases made over the internet, or as part of the 4- and 5-Park Orlando Flex Tickets 🍴 Makahiki Luau, Dine With Shamu, Sharks Underwater Grill ($$$), reservations ☎ 1-800 327 2424. Also assorted cafés, snack, BBQ and sandwich shops 🚌 I-Ride, Lynx #42

47

# Silver Springs

www.silversprings.com

Boat trips, jeep safaris, animal encounters and popular music shows are all part of the deal at "Florida's Original Attraction."

In 1878, Silver Springs entrepreneur Hullam Jones had a brainwave. He installed a glass viewing box in the flat bottom of a dugout canoe and invented the glass-bottomed boat tour, hence this popular nature park's claim to being the Sunshine State's first tourist attraction.

More than a century on, the glass-bottomed boat rides are as popular as ever, creating a window into an underwater world teeming with fish, turtles, crustaceans and ancient fossils at the head of the world's largest artesian spring formation. You can also enjoy the Lost River Voyage that plies the unspoilt Silver River, with a stop at a wildlife rescue outpost; or a Jungle Cruise on Fort King Waterway, where non-native animals look on. Jeep safaris also do the jungle thing, four-wheeling through a 35-acre (14-ha) Florida jungle, with specially designed animal habitats like Big Gator Lagoon.

Showtime at Silver Springs brings on the bugs and the creepy-crawlies at Creature Feature, an alarmingly up-close look at spiders and scorpions, toads and giant Madagascan hissing cockroaches. For something a little more wholesome, watch domestic cats and dogs performing tricks at the Amazing Pets displays. The park also attracts popular music acts for its annual weekend Concert Series (included with admission) starting in March.

BEST PLACES TO SEE

🕂 *25f (off map)* ✉ SR40, 1 mile (1.61km) east of Ocala (72 miles/116km northwest of Orlando) ☎ 352/236-2121 🕓 Daily 10–5 (extended summer and hols) ✋ Very expensive 🍴 The Deli ($); Springside Pizzeria ($); Springside Restaurant ($–$$); Swampy's Smokehouse Buffet ($–$$); snack stops, ice cream and cold drinks stalls ($)

BEST PLACES TO SEE

8 Wet 'n Wild

www.wetnwildorlando.com

If the beach is too far, Wet 'n Wild is a perfect – and in some ways much more exciting – alternative

When it opened in 1977, Wet 'n Wild set the standard for the elaborate water park. There was more than simply a few slides here; there were

BEST PLACES TO SEE

twisting, barreling, churning rapids as well as innovative watery rides, wide beaches, a surf lagoon, restaurants, picnic areas and a lazy river. The park, located on International Drive, is hugely popular from April to October, with the peak season running from June through August.

You will be astonished at the ingenuity that has gone into creating heart-stopping thrill rides. For instance, the Black Hole sends you shooting 500ft (152m) down a spinning, twisting, dark tunnel, forced through by a gusher of water. Der Stuka is one of the highest, fastest waterslides in the world. One of the scariest attractions is Bomb Bay. Step into a large enclosed cylinder, cross your arms and legs, and then the floor below you drops out to send you sliding on a 76-ft (23-m) vertical free fall before you slip into a curve to slow your descent. Kids are catered to with a separate area featuring thrilling kid-sized rides and attractions.

You don't have to be a thrillseeker to enjoy Wet 'n Wild; there are plenty of more peaceful offerings. You can bring picnic lunches and coolers with food into the park, the pools are heated, as many as 400 lifeguards are on duty in peak season, and this is one of the rare water parks opened year-round.

✚ 8F ✉ 6200 International Drive (1–4/Exit 75AB)
☎ 407/351-1800 or 1-800 992 WILD (9453) ⏰ Daily 10–5 (extending 9–9 or later in summer) 👋 Very expensive
🍴 Surf Grill ($–$$); Bubba's BBQ & Chicken ($–$$); Manny's Pizza & Subs ($–$$); Cookies & Cones ($) 🚌 I-Ride, Lynx 42

BEST PLACES TO SEE

9 Walt Disney World Resort®

www.disneyworld.com

This is the big one: Walt Disney's Florida showcase put Orlando on the map and has become a legend in its own short lifetime.

Walt Disney World® Resort is the largest and most famous theme park resort in the world. Its 27,500-acre (11,134-ha) site is twice the size of Manhattan, and although only a small portion of this has been developed to date, it has four major theme parks: Magic Kingdom®, Epcot®, Disney's Hollywood Studios (formerly Disney-MGM Studios) and Disney's Animal Kingdom® Park, plus two water parks, a nightclub area within the huge lakefront Downtown Disney® shopping, dining and entertainment district, themed resorts, gardens, golf courses and a professional sports complex.

Walt Disney opened his first theme park in Anaheim, California, in 1955. Disneyland, the prototype for the Magic Kingdom® (which now flourishes in Japan, France and Hong Kong, as well as Florida) was a huge success, but Disney was unable to control the explosion of hotels that popped up around the site and prevented him from expanding the park. Instead, he looked for alternative spots and was drawn to Orlando for its climate, communications links and vast tracts of cheap farmland, which

© Disney

BEST PLACES TO SEE

© Disney

he began to purchase in secret during 1964. With 27,500 acres (11,134ha) in the bag at a cost of about $5.5 million, Disney announced his plans to create "a complete vacation environment".

Disney died in 1966 without seeing his Florida vision completed. But The Walt Disney Company did him proud, producing Magic Kingdom® in Disneyland's image. This opened in 1971, followed by Epcot® in 1982, then Disney-MGM Studios was rushed out in 1989, months ahead of Universal Studios' mammoth Florida facility (➤ 54–55). Now Central Florida's animal-orientated parks are feeling the pinch as Disney's Animal Kingdom® Park exercises its powerful Disney appeal on the public.

"Doing Disney" is quite an undertaking. Take a tip from the repeat visitors who plan their itineraries with almost military precision, zero in on the best rides and avoid the restaurants at peak times. Never plan on doing more than one park a day, and if you are visiting all four parks include at least one rest day. See also ➤ 149–185.

✚ 4C ✉ Walt Disney World® Resort, Lake Buena Vista (US 192 and several exits off I-4, 20 miles/32km south of Orlando) ☎ 407/824-4321 ⓘ Check current schedules ✋ Very expensive 🚌 Free shuttle bus services from many Orlando/Kissimmee hotels ❓ Details of daily parades, showtimes and nighttime displays are printed in current park guides. Tickets are available on a one-day, one-park basis. For longer stay guests, a choice of multi-day passes offer greater flexibility and savings. They cover unlimited admission to any combination of theme parks, WDW Resort transportation, and limited admission to other Disney attractions. Unused days expire 14 days after activation

BEST PLACES TO SEE

10 Universal Orlando® Resort

www.universalorlando.com

Blockbuster rides, shows and attractions recreate movie magic and comic strip heroes at Universal's two Florida theme parks.

Disney may have greater worldwide recognition, but for many visitors to Orlando – particularly adult and teenage thrillseekers – Universal delivers a more exciting theme park experience. The original, movie-orientated, Universal Studios® Florida theme park opened in 1990, sharing a site with the largest working movie and television production facility outside Hollywood. It soon developed a worldwide reputation for innovative, state-of-the-art thrill rides. Recently the excellent and extremely popular Shrek 4-D™, Revenge of the Mummy℠ – The Ride and newly opened Simpsons ride have added three brand new reasons to visit Universal.

In 1999, Universal Studios® Florida metamorphosed into Universal Orlando® Resort, a complete resort destination with on-site hotels, the 30-acre (12-ha) Universal CityWalk® shopping, dining and entertainment complex, and a second theme park, Universal's Islands of Adventure®. Adrenaline junkies are in for a treat at Islands of Adventure®, which styles its roller-coaster and thrill rides after Marvel comic book heroes such as Spider-Man, Doctor Doom and the Incredible Hulk. A further range of rides and shows features the likes of Sinbad the Sailor, Jurassic Park's dinosaurs and children's favorites Dr Seuss and Popeye.

BEST PLACES TO SEE

After dark, all the action moves to CityWalk®, which boasts the world's biggest Hard Rock Café, attached to a 2,200-seat auditorium, a movie megaplex, shopping, nightclubs, jazz, and a wide variety of themed restaurants, ranging from a NASCAR Café for motorsports fans to a very laidback Key West-styled Jimmy Buffett's Margaritaville. See also ➤ 88–97.

✚ 16H ✉ 1000 Universal Orlando Plaza, Orlando (I-4/Exit 74B or 75A) ☎ 407/363-8000 or 1-800 232 7827 🕐 Daily from 9am; closing times vary ✋ Very expensive 🍴 Both parks offer a choice of dining options, from snack stops and counter service cafés to full restaurants

55

Best things to do

Best theme park restaurants	58–59
Good places to cool off	60–61
A drive around Mount Dora	62–63
Great dinner shows	64–65
Free attractions	66–67
Top golf courses	68–69
Spectator sports	70–71

57

BEST THINGS TO DO

Best theme park restaurants

Brown Derby
Cool and clubby replica of Hollywood moguls' meeting place. Pasta, steaks, Cobb salad.
✉ Disney' Hollywood Studios ☎ 407/939-3463

Les Chefs de France
Elegant Disney outpost for French *nouvelle cuisine*.
✉ Epcot® ☎ 407/939-3463

Coral Reef
First-class seafood and a stunning view of the coral reef exhibition.
✉ Epcot® ☎ 407/939-3463

Crown Colony
Family restaurant overlooking the animals of the Serengeti Plain exhibit. Chicken dinners, fresh seafood, sandwiches.
✉ Busch Gardens, Tampa ☎ 1-888 800 5447

Emeril's Orlando
Chef Emeril Lagasse's upscale and elegant restaurant serving such delights as pan-seared grouper, sauteed shrimp and baked Maine lobster.
✉ Universal CityWalk® ☎ 407/224-2424

Hard Rock Café
Big fun, big name rock memorabilia and big burgers.
✉ Universal CityWalk® ☎ 407/351-7625

Liberty Tree Tavern
All-American home-style cooking in a re-created colonial inn. Turkey dinners, Cape Cod pasta, pot roast.
✉ Magic Kingdom® ☎ 407/939-3463

BEST THINGS TO DO

Lombard's Seafood Grill
Seafood specialties, pasta and steaks, plus waterfront dining in the re-created San Francisco district.
✉ Universal Studios® ☎ 407/224-6401

Makahiki Luau
Dinner-only South Seas feast and entertainment (call ahead to make reservations).
✉ SeaWorld ☎ 1-800 327 2424

Sharks Underwater Grill
Fresh fish and Floribbean cuisine.
✉ SeaWorld ☎ 407/351-3600

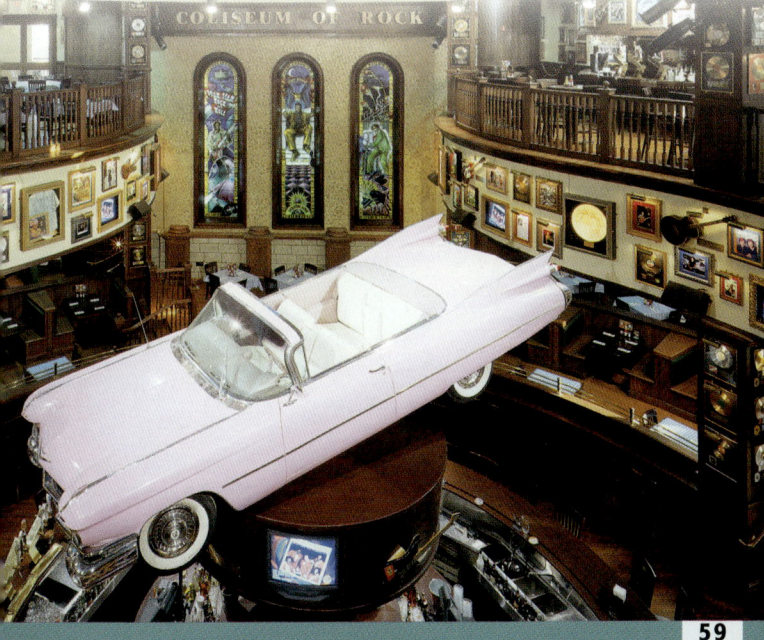

BEST THINGS TO DO

Good places to cool off

Blizzard Beach (➤ 153) is a Disney water park with a ski resort theme, where the chair lifts lead to water slides surrounding Mount Gushmore.

Blue Spring (➤ 120–121) is a popular swimming hole for snorkeling, scuba diving or just splashing around.

Canaveral National Seashore offers miles of unspoilt seashore and beaches north of the Kennedy Space Center.

Central Florida Springs (➤ 132–133) make perfect swimming holes, set in the tranquil state parks.

Cocoa Beach is one of Florida's famous "party" beaches on the Atlantic Coast, an hour's drive down the Bee Line Expressway/SR528.

Tanganyika Tidal Wave at Busch Gardens (➤ 118) makes a big splash with visitors and cools off onlookers and riders alike.

Typhoon Lagoon (➤ 176) is an impressive water park with a Shark Reef, whitewater rafting adventure, flumes and water slides.

Wekiwa Springs is a lovely woodland park, with swimming and canoeing beneath huge oak and cypress trees.

Wet 'n Wild (➤ 50–51) is an elaborate water park with heart-stopping thrill rides.

Wild Waters (➤ 134) is a relaxing water park adjacent to Silver Springs, with a wave pool, water slides and flume rides.

BEST THINGS TO DO

BEST THINGS TO DO

a drive around Mount Dora

A pretty lakeshore town set amid gently rolling countryside and citrus groves, Mount Dora is renowned for its Victorian architecture and antiques shops.

From Orlando, take the Orange Blossom Trail/US441 north (direction Ocala) to Mount Dora, and follow signs for downtown.

Northern settlers first arrived on the shores of Lake Dora in the 1870s, and built their town on a low rise overlooking the eastern end of lake. The oldest surviving building in town is the 1883 Lakeside Inn, 100 Alexander Street, a short step away from the Chamber of Commerce.

At the Chamber of Commerce, 341 Alexander Street (C352/383-2165), pick up a driving map indicating a 3-mile (5-km) route around the pick of Mount Dora's historic homes.

62

BEST THINGS TO DO

The attractively restored downtown district is fun to explore within the Historic Shopping Village; many of the old buildings house art galleries, specialty gift stores, tempting gourmet food emporiums and popular antiques shops. Also in downtown is Mount Dora's most impressive historic home, the splendid Queen Anne-style Donnelly House. Ornately decorated with ironwork, a cupola, copious gables, balustrades, balconies and yards of gingerbread trim, it now serves as probably the daintiest Masonic Hall in the land. Nearby, the town's former fire station and jail houses the small Royellou Museum, displaying local history exhibits. By the lake there is a nature trail in Palm Island Park; boats and bicycles are available to rent. It's a touch of New England in the heart of Florida.

Return to Orlando on the US441 or SR46/I-4.

Distance 60-mile (97-km) round trip
Time A 50-minute drive from Orlando. Allow half a day to look around Mount Dora
Start/end point Orlando
Destination Mount Dora
Lunch Windsor Rose English Tea Room ($) ✉ 142 W 4th Avenue
☎ 352/735-2551

BEST THINGS TO DO

Great dinner shows

ORLANDO
Dolly Parton's Dixie Stampede
The legendary country siren lent her name to promote this down-home dinner show near Disney. The theme is North vs. South showdown centered around horse racing, stunts and lots of music. Great southern cooking – that you'll eat minus untensils.
✉ 8251 Vineland Avenue ☎ 866/443-4943; www.dixiestampede.com
🕒 Check website for schedule

Pirate's Dinner Adventure
Yo ho ho and a suitably piratical dinner show with a motley crew of entertainers and a post-show Buccaneer Bash.
✉ 6400 Carrier Drive (off International Drive) ☎ 407/248-0590 or 1-800 866 2469; www.piratesdinneradventure.com 🕒 Nightly

Sleuths Mystery Dinner Shows
Solve a whodunnit between courses at this small dinner attraction. Entertaining action with a comedy angle. The second seating can be overly long.
✉ 7508 Universal Boulevard ☎ 407/363-1985; www.sleuth.com
🕒 Nightly

KISSIMMEE
Arabian Nights
A spectacular equestrian dinner attraction, with over $5 million-worth of prime horseflesh and enough glitz to rival Las Vegas. Good family entertainment.
✉ 6225 W Irlo Bronson Memorial Highway/US192 (GM 8)
☎ 407/239-9223 or 1-800 553 6116; www.arabiannights.com
🕒 Nightly

Capone's
An intimate 1930s speakeasy is the setting for this gangsters-and-molls comedy musical show. The small cast

BEST THINGS TO DO

throws itself into the dance numbers with enthusiasm.
✉ 4740 W Irlo Bronson Memorial Highway/US192 (GM 12.5) ☎ 407/397-2378 or 1-800 220 8428; www.alcapones.com ⏰ Nightly

Medieval Times
An evening of medieval spectator sports as dashing knights take part in action-packed horseback games of skill and daring, jousting and sword fights.
✉ 4510 W Irlo Bronson Memorial Highway/US192 (GM 14.5) ☎ 407/396-2900 or 1-888 935 6878; www.medievaltimes.com ⏰ Nightly

WALT DISNEY WORLD® RESORT AND LAKE BUENA VISTA

Disney's Spirit of Aloha
Open-air tropical feast at the Polynesian Resort where you dine on foods inspired by the South Seas: lanai-roasted chicken and barbecue ribs in a beachside cabana. Hula lessons included.
✉ Disney's Polynesian Resort, 1600 Seven Seas Drive ☎ 407/939-3463; http://disneyworld.disney.go.com ⏰ Nightly

Hoop-Dee Doo Musical Revue
Popular Disney country-style hoe-down with sing-along tunes and a good all-you-can-eat barbecue.
✉ Disney's Fort Wilderness Resort, 4510 N Fort Wilderness Trail ☎ 407/939-3463; http://disneyworld.disney.go.com ⏰ Nightly

BEST THINGS TO DO

Free attractions

Audubon's Center for Birds of Prey
Aviaries housing birds of prey, including eagles, owls and hawks.
✉ 1101 Audubon Way, Maitland ☎ 407/644-0190
✋ A $5 donation is appreciated

Bradlee-McIntyre House
Orange County's only Victorian cottage.
✉ 130 W Warren Avenue (at CR427), Longwood
☎ 407/332-0225

Fort Christmas Park
Replica fort, pioneer homes and Seminole War exhibits.
✉ 1300 Fort Christmas Road, Christmas ☎ 407/568-4149

Lake Eola Park
Downtown's lakeside park with picnicking areas, children's play-ground and boat rentals.
✉ Eola Drive, Orlando ☎ 407/246-282

Kraft Azalea Gardens
Azaleas, subtropical plants and cypress trees on shore of Lake Maitland.
✉ Alabama Drive, Winter Park ☎ 407/599-3334

Lakeridge Winery & Vineyards
Guided tours and tastings.
✉ 19239 N US27, Clermont ☎ 352/394-8627 or 1-800 768 9463

West Orange Trail
A 4.5-mile (7km) trail for walkers, cyclists and skaters (bicycle and skate rental available) from

BEST THINGS TO DO

Killarnet Station to downtown. It is part of a longer trail whose total length is 22 miles. For more information visit www.orangecountyparks.net

✉ Winter Garden
☎ 407/877-0600

Zora Neale Hurston National Museum of Fine Arts
Exhibits by artists of African descent in Zora Neale Hurston's home town.

✉ 227 E Kennedy Boulevard, Eatonville ☎ 407/647-3307

Festivals
Check out the great variety of festivals and events going on around the area nearly every month of the year. They feature music, arts, crafts, food, fireworks and entertainment. Many take place on the banks of Lake Eola in downtown Orlando or at Lakefront park in Kissimmee.

BEST THINGS TO DO

Top golf courses

Arnold Palmer Golf Academy
There are programs for all ages and levels of experience to learn the fundamentals or enhance your game. The stunning Bay Hill course has 27 holes along the shores of the Butler Chain of Lakes.
✉ 9000 Bay Hill Boulevard, Orlando ☎ 407/876-5362

Black Bear Golf Club
Surrounded by many lakes and horse farms, this beautiful 18-hole course north of Orlando has rolling hills with panoramic views.
✉ 24505 Calusa Boulevard, Eustis ☎ 352/357-4732 or 1-800 423 2718

Celebration Golf Club
Two highly-rated, challenging 18-hole championship golf courses designed by Robert Trent Jones Sr and Jr.
✉ 701 Golf Park Drive, Celebration ☎ 407/566-4653

Disney's Palm and Magnolia Golf Courses
Scene of the Walt Disney World® Golf Classic tournament, these two championship courses have received four-star ratings from Golf Digest magazine.
✉ Walt Disney World® Resort, Lake Buena Vista ☎ 407/939-4653

© Disney

BEST THINGS TO DO

Faldo Golf Institute by Marriott
One of the largest golf learning centers in the country, with more than 100 hitting stations and a challenging 9-hole course.
✉ 12001 Avenida Verde, Orlando ☎ 407/238-7677

Grand Cypress
This premier Jack Nicklaus signature-designed golf course offers three 9-hole courses and one 18-hole course which was modeled after the Scottish Links courses such as St Andrews, with pot bunkers, stone walls and other features.
✉ Grand Cypress Resort, North Jacaranda, Orlando ☎ 407/239-1904

MetroWest Golf Club
Located 2 miles north of Universal Studios, this championship course, designed by Robert Trent Jones Sr, is one of the best public golf courses in the city.
✉ 2100 S Hiawassee Road, Orlando ☎ 407/299-1099

Orange County National Golf Center
Two championship courses, Panther Lake and Crooked Cat, play host to PGA Tour events.
✉ 16301 Phil Ritson Way, Winter Garden ☎ 407/656-2626 or 1-888 727 3672

Stoneybrook Golf Club
Beautiful championship golf course with tree-lined fairways and strategic carries over preserved wetlands and waterways. Its sister club, Stoneybrook West, is in Winter Garden.
✉ 2900 Northampton Avenue, Orlando ☎ 407/384-6888

Timacuan Golf & Country Club
One of the top-ranked courses in the state, with a spectacular par 71 championship course and a flood-lit driving range.
✉ 550 Timacuan Boulevard, Lake Mary ☎ 407/321-0010

Spectator sports

AMERICAN FOOTBALL
Orlando Predators
Aspiring local Arena Football League competitors. Check listings in the local papers for details of upcoming games.
✉ TD Waterhouse Centre, 600 W Amelia Street ☎ 407/648-4444

BASEBALL
Atlanta Braves
At Disney's Wide World of Sports® complex, the Braves play their spring training games against other pro teams in a brand-new, old-fashioned stadium where you can spread out a blanket on the lawn and watch professional players up close.
✉ Walt Disney World® Resort ☎ 407/939-1500

Osceola County Stadium & Sports Complex
Spring training home of the Houston Astros and host to many amateur and professional baseball events throughout the year.
✉ 631 Heritage Parkway (off E US192), Kissimmee ☎ 321/697-3200; www.orlandosports.org

BASKETBALL
Orlando Magic
Downtown TD Waterhouse Centre is home to the local Eastern Division NBA contenders when they are in town. Season October to April or May, reservations advised.
✉ TD Waterhouse Centre, 600 W Amelia Street ☎ 407/896-2442 or 1-800 338 0005 ❓ Tickets from 1-888-622 6444 or 407/916-2969; www.orlandomagic.com

Orlando Miracle
When the Magic are taking a summer break, the Miracle women's NBA professionals provide fun family sporting entertainment.
✉ TD Waterhouse Centre, 600 W Amelia Street ☎ 407/916-2969

GOLF
PGA Events
Orlando is Florida's golfing capital. Local courses host two annual PGA events: in Mar, the Arnold Palmer Invitational, formerly known as the Bay Hill Invitational is played at the Arnold Palmer Golf Academy (✉ 9000 Bay Hill Boulevard, Orlando ☎ 407/876-2888, www.bayhill.com); in Oct, Disney offers a million-dollar purse for the Walt Disney World® Resort Classic, played on its Magnolia and Palm courses (☎ 407/939-2272, www.disneyworld.com).

MOTOR RACING
Daytona International Speedway
Home to the famous Daytona 500 (February) and the Pepsi 400 NASCAR Nextel Cup Series races (July), plus the Biketoberfest (October) motorcycle events.
✉ 1801 W International Speedway Boulevard ☎ 386/253-RACE (7223); www.daytonainternationalspeedway.com

SPORTS COMPLEX
Disney's Wide World of Sports® Complex
Disney's spectacular 200-acre (81-ha) sporting venue boasts world-class facilities for more than 30 sports, a speedway, and hosts national and international events.
✉ Lake Buena Vista ☎ 407/939-1500; www.disneyworldsports.com
🕐 Open for events only, hours vary

Exploring

| Orlando | 75–112 |

| Around Orlando | 113–148 |

| Walt Disney World® Resort | 149–185 |

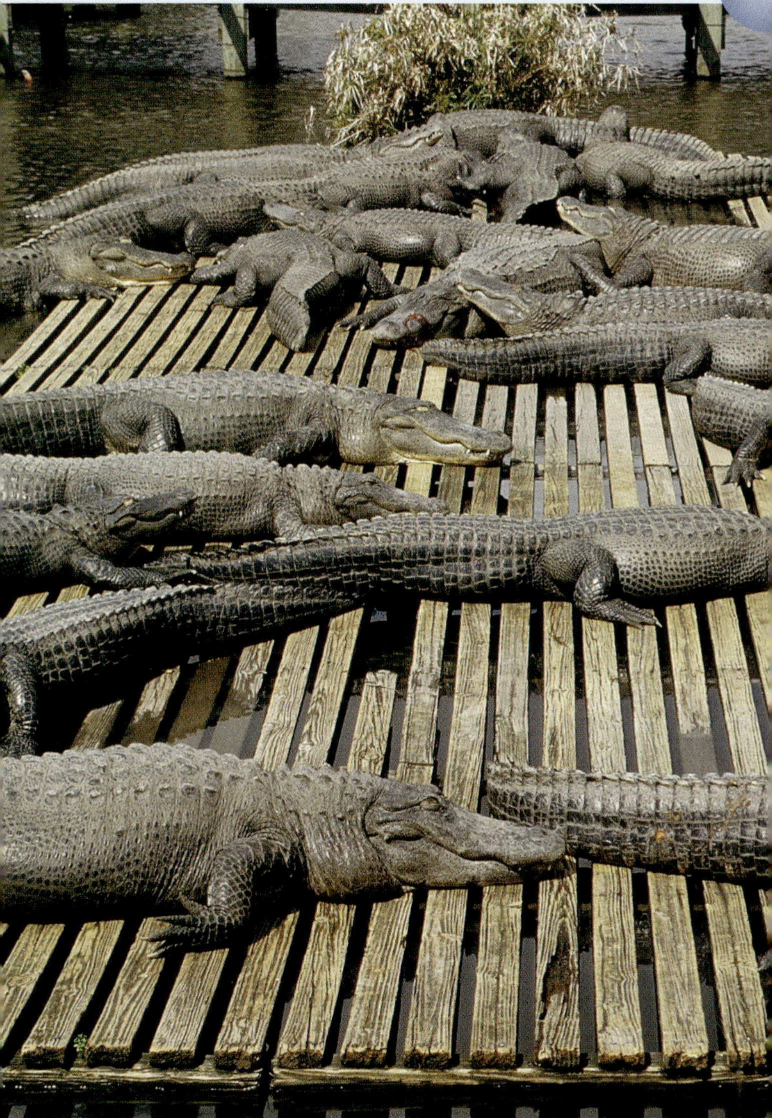

EXPLORING

In the 1930s, traffic signals in downtown Orlando wore a sign admonishing drivers to be quiet. There were fresh fruit juice stands on the sidewalk and the city resembled "a great, cultivated park." Since Orlando has become synonymous with theme parks, it is generally assumed to be a loud, brash place. Living in the shadow of the Mouse has certainly brought radical changes. The mini-Manhattan of the downtown district is bounded by highways, and the sky is busy with jets coming to and going from the international airport. But the city of Orlando has not succumbed entirely to the trappings of the tourist industry. There are pockets of greenery in Lake Eola and Harry P Leu Gardens, and recent developments have included the renovated historic district around Downtown, the Orlando Science Center and its satellite art and history museums, and the palatial Orange County Convention Center.

Orlando

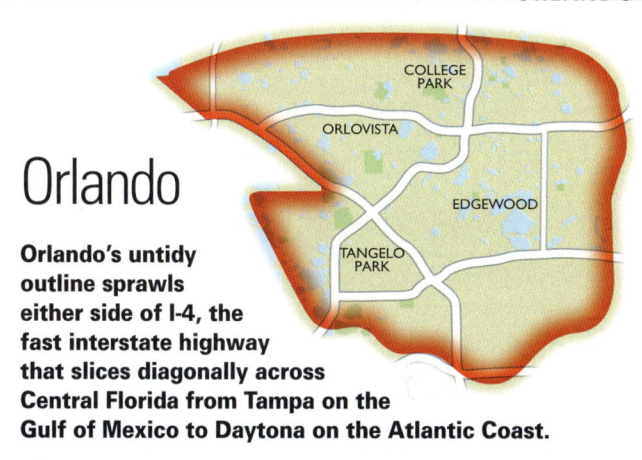

Orlando's untidy outline sprawls either side of I-4, the fast interstate highway that slices diagonally across Central Florida from Tampa on the Gulf of Mexico to Daytona on the Atlantic Coast.

The city has extended steadily southwest towards Walt Disney World® Resort and Kissimmee, and most visitors who stay in Orlando are based south of the city in the International Drive resort area. SeaWorld, Discovery Cove and Universal Orlando are just off I-Drive (as International Drive is familiarly called), which is served by the I-Ride trolley.

It may come as a suprise to the vast majority of visitors who never venture beyond the distinctly touristy environs of I-Drive and the major theme parks, but Orlando does have more to offer than the well-traveled strip of hotels, motels, discount malls and smaller attractions that constitute the city's main resort area.

EXPLORING

DISCOVERY COVE
Best places to see, ➤ 40–41.

GATORLAND
Southeast of Orlando, on the border with Kissimmee, a pair of giant alligator jaws forms the entrance to this classic Florida attraction. Hundreds of captive "gators" occupy various pens and pools. There are alligator shows, alligator meals (try Gator Nuggets in Pearl's Smokehouse), and alligator products, such as wallets, boots and handbags, on sale in the gift shop. Other Gatorland residents include Florida crocodiles and caymans, native snapping and soft-shell turtles, and snake displays feature venomous rattlesnakes and cottonmouth moccasins.

ORLANDO

A highlight is the 2,000-ft (610-m) long marshland boardwalk edging a cypress swamp. This is a native habitat alligator breeding ground and a great birdwatching spot. In spring, snowy egrets construct their nests within a few feet of passers-by, and there are great and little blue herons, pigeon-sized little green herons and dozens of other wading birds.

www.gatorland.com

✚ 11A ✉ 14501 S Orange Blossom Trail ☎ 407/855-5496 or 1-800 393 5297 ◷ Daily 9am–dusk ✋ Expensive 🍴 Pearl's Smokehouse ($)

HARRY P LEU GARDENS
Best places to see, ➤ 42–43.

EXPLORING

HERITAGE SQUARE
A focus for downtown Orlando, the Heritage Square development has been designed to symbolize "the heart of the community." This is the site where the city's early pioneers would have plotted out the land and planned its development. The old Orange County Courthouse is here, which houses the Orange County Regional History Center (➤ 79), and the almost 2-acre (1-ha) park and plaza has been attractively landscaped with native trees, plants and Floridian-inspired landmarks as well as a pop-jet fountain that is a magnet for children.

✚ 21K ✉ Central Boulevard at Magnolia Avenue (I-4 to exit 82C/Anderson Street)

MENNELLO MUSEUM
Florida's only folk art museum is a delightful find for fans of the genre. The works of Earl Cunningham (1893–1977) form the basis of the collections courtesy of Florida collectors Michael and Marilyn Mennello, who are donating 44 of Cunningham's works to the museum over 13 years. Cunningham, who could list chicken farmer, seaman and junk dealer among his former careers, favored "historical-fantasy" themes and his colorful palette adapts superbly to exuberant depictions of typically Floridian scenes from florious technicolor sunsets and native birdlife to Seminole villages and lively marine paintings featuring his favorite early 20th-century schooners. The museum also hosts regular visiting exhibitions of modern and antique paintings and sculpture.

www.mennellomuseum.org
✚ 21M ✉ 900 E Princeton Street (I-4 to exit 85) ☎ 407/246-4278
🕐 Tue–Sat 10:30–4:30, Sun 12–4:30 ✋ Inexpensive

ORANGE COUNTY REGIONAL HISTORY CENTER

Unfortunately, many visitors believe Florida was discovered by Walt Disney. At this first-class museum, historians try to set the record straight by focusing on the people and society that existed in the pre-theme park years. In the handsomely restored 1927 Orange County Courthouse, the Center recalls Central Florida history through imaginative audio and visual presentations as well as hands-on exhibits. You are greeted by The Dome, a three-dimensional showcase for Florida icons, followed by an orientation experience. Suitably immersed in local lore, exhibits whisk you back in time to the Paleo-Indian era and a Timucuan village, the arrival of the Spanish explorers, a pioneer Cracker homestead, and the Roaring 20s when Tin Can tourists in Model-T Fords descended on Florida in their thousands.

www.thehistorycenter.org
✚ 21K ✉ One Heritage Square, 65 E Central Boulevard (I-4 to Exit 82C/Anderson Street)
☎ 407/836-8500 or 1-800 965 2030 🕐 Mon–Sat 10–5, Sun 12–5 ✋ Inexpensive

EXPLORING

ORLANDO MUSEUM OF ART
The museum invites tourists to experience Orlando's cultural side and often hosts touring exhibitions, so check current schedules. If the permanent collections are on show, visitors will be rewarded with a notable collection of pre-Columbian art – some 250 pieces dating from around 1200BC to AD1500 – plus works by leading 19th- to 20th-century American artists and African art exhibits.
www.omart.org

✚ 21M ✉ Loch Haven Park, 2416 North Mills Avenue at E Princeton Street (I-4/Exit 85) ☎ 407/896-4231 🕐 Tue–Fri 10–4, Sat–Sun 12–4 ✋ Moderate

ORLANDO SCIENCE CENTER
Topped by a distinctive silver observatory dome, Orlando's impressive Science Center opened its doors in 1997. The exhibits are laid out over four levels and include dozens of interactive displays and hands-on educational games designed to appeal to children of all ages – and not a few adults as well.

On ground level, the NatureWorks Florida habitat section combines models and living exhibits such as turtles, baby alligators and a reef tank, and there is the excellent KidsTown early learning

ORLANDO

area for 8s and under. On Levels 2, 3 and 4, more elaborate and sophisticated exhibits tackle the basics of physics, mathematics, applied technologies and human biology in comprehensible and entertaining style. Movie moguls should definitely see the TechWorks exhibit on Level 4, which explores the behind-the-scenes tricks of the movie trade.

In addition, there are daily science-orientated shows in the Darden Adventure Theater and the Digistar Planetarium, and large format film presentations in the CineDome, which boasts a massive 8,000sq-ft (732sq-m) IMAX screen. On Friday and Saturday nights, while the CineDome features 3-D laser light shows, the Observatory welcomes stargazers.

www.osc.org

🚆 21M ✉ 777 E Princeton Street (I-4/Exit 85) ☎ 407/514-2000 or 1-888 672 4386 🕒 Sun–Thu 10–6, Fri–Sat 10–9 💰 Moderate 🍴 OSC Cafe ($)

EXPLORING

RIPLEY'S BELIEVE IT OR NOT! ORLANDO ODDITORIUM

A whacky, lop-sided building tipping down an imaginary sinkhole, a hologram greeting from the long-dead Robert L Ripley and hundreds of curious, eccentric and downright bizarre exhibits add up to a fairly unbelievable attraction. Robert Ripley was a connoisseur of oddities. Traveling extensively in the 1920s and 1930s, he amassed enough material to stock more than a dozen "museums" of this type worldwide. Typical exhibits include a Mona Lisa made from 1,426 squares of toast and a three-quarter scale model of a 1907 Rolls Royce Silver Ghost made out of 1,016,711 matchsticks and 63 pints of glue.

✚ 8E ✉ 8201 International Drive ☎ 407/345-0501 or 1-800 998 4418 ⏰ Daily 9am–1am 💰 Expensive
🚌 I-Ride, Lynx #42

ORLANDO

SEAWORLD ORLANDO

SeaWorld's well-balanced combination of sights and shows is a proven winner. Unlike some parks, where the shows are incidental to the main action, here they are an intrinsic ingredient, and the rest of the attractions – plus behind-the-scenes tours – can be fitted in as visitors make their way around the many and various show stadiums.

Unusual dining options in the park include Dine with Shamu and the classy Sharks Underwater Grill. Sunset reveals another side of SeaWorld, with nightly laser and fireworks displays and the Makahiki Luau Dinner and Show. Below is a list of highlights; see also ➤ 46–47.

Sea Lion and Otter Stadium

Sea lions, otters and lumbering walruses are incorporated in the melodramatic swashbuckling tale, "Clyde and Seamore Take Pirate Island." Weaving cute tricks into the story highlights the animal attraction.

Journey to Atlantis

Rickety Greek fishing boats transport guests on a sightseeing trip to the newly risen City of Atlantis when disaster strikes and a high-speed water ride with special effects ensues.

EXPLORING

Key West at SeaWorld
A Florida Keys themed area, with a tropical atmosphere and street performers. The centerpiece is 2-acre (1-ha) Dolphin Cove, a lagoon habitat for Atlantic bottlenose dolphins adjacent to the Whale & Dolphin Stadium. Rescued turtles bask on the rocks of Turtle Point, visitors can feed and pet captive stingrays in the Stingray Lagoon, and there are nightly festivities in Sunset Square.

Kraken
More thrills aboard a mega sea serpent-styled roller-coaster.

Manatee Rescue
A distant aquatic relative of the elephant, the manatee is now a seriously endangered species. There may be fewer than 2,000 of these giant Florida sea cows left in the wild. All the manatees in this SeaWorld exhibit are rescued and will be returned to the wild if possible.

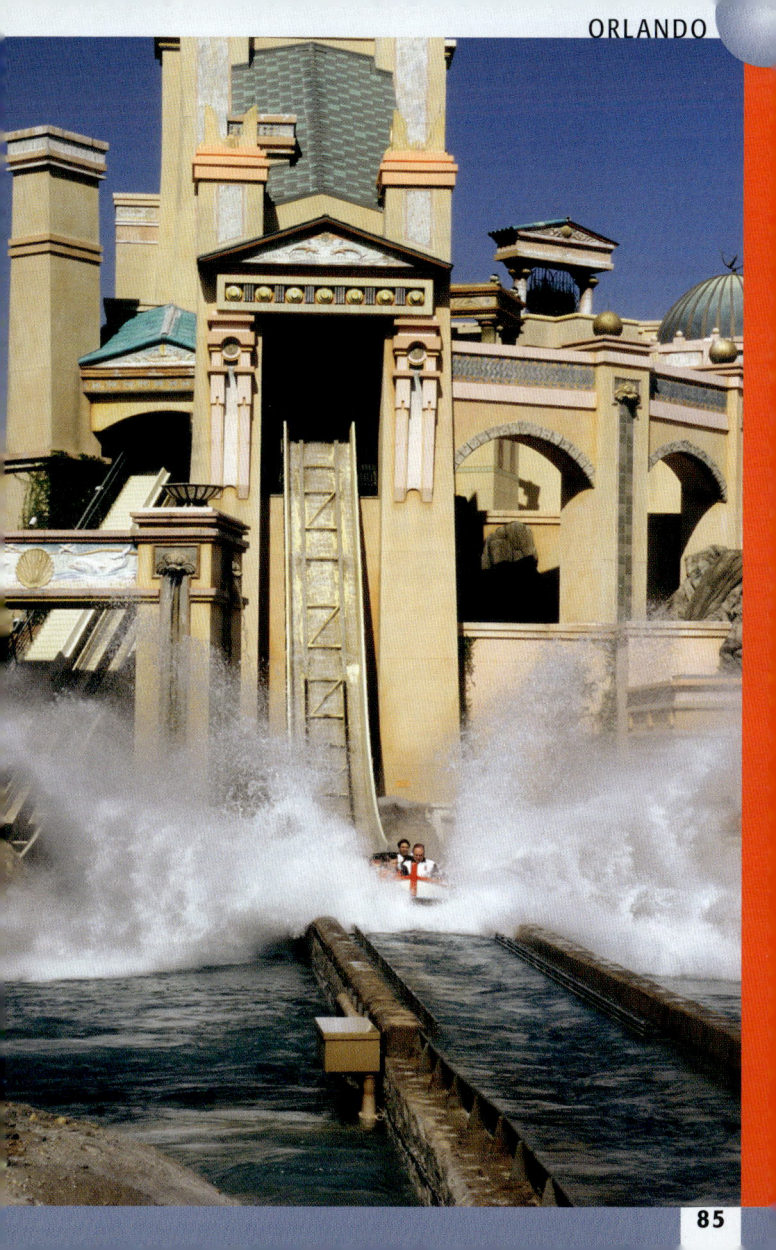

ORLANDO

EXPLORING

Pacific Point Preserve
California sea lions, harbor seals and South American fur seals occupy this rocky northern Pacific coast re-creation, complete with wave machine.

Penguin Encounter
Some 200 enchanting Antarctic penguins and their Arctic cousins, the alcids (better known as puffins and mures), inhabit these icy confines.

Shamu Adventure
An introduction to the world of the killer whale hosted by animal expert Jack Hanna. Makes a good preface to the Shamu stadium shows.

Shamu's Happy Harbor
Play area for small children with climbing apparatus, radio-controlled boats, a sandpit and face-painting activities.

Terrors of the Deep
Scene-setting, spooky music and eerie lighting accompany these aquariums full of lurking moray eels, 28-mph (45-kph) barracudas and highly toxic puffer fish. Ride the perspex tunnel through the 660,000-gal shark tank, or get really up close and personal with the park's daring interaction program, Sharks Deep Dive, and don a wetsuit for a ride through the habitat in a shark cage.

Wild Arctic

A simulated helicopter ride transports visitors to an Arctic base station for close encounters with polar bears, beluga whales and walruses. However, the icy habitats appear distinctly cramped for these large animals.

www.seaworld.com

✚ 8D ✉ 7007 SeaWorld Drive, Orlando (I-4/Exit 71 or72) ☎ 407/351-3600 or 1-800 432 1178 🕐 Daily 9–7 (extended summer and hols) 👍 Orlando FlexTickets offer reduced rates and flexibility. Available from participating parks, 4-Park tickets provide unlimited admission to SeaWorld Orlando, Universal Orlando and Wet 'n Wild. 5-Park tickets include Busch Gardens in Tampa 🍴 Several restaurants and snack stops. Reservations for Dine With Shamu, Sharks Underwater Grill and Makahiki Luau should be made in advance on ☎ 1-800 327 2424 🚌 I-Ride, Lynx #42 ❓ Guided tours of Terrors of the Deep, Wild Arctic and the animal rescue and research facility can be made at the Guided Tours counter near the entrance. For Sharks Deep Dive, the Beluga Interaction Program, Marine Mammal Keeper plus the guided Adventure Express Tour of the park, advance reservations are recommended, ☎ 1-800 432 1178 (press 5)

EXPLORING

UNIVERSAL ORLANDO® RESORT
See pages 54–55 and information under Universal Studios® and Universal's Islands of Adventure®.

UNIVERSAL STUDIOS®
It would be a mistake to assume that if you have done Disney's Hollywood Studios (▶ 157–159) you should skip this. The Universal experience is more ride-orientated than its Disney rival and the attractive layout is a definite plus. The most popular shows on the Universal lot include the Beetlejuice's Graveyard Revue™;

ORLANDO

Blues Brothers® soul-style entertainment; and Animal Actors On Location!™ showcasing talented animals. Below is a list of highlights.

Earthquake®
It is a short step off the San Francisco street set to this subway journey from hell. Experience an 8.3 on the Richter Scale, as portrayed in the classic 1974 disaster movie *Earthquake*.

ET Adventure®
A gentle ride over 3,340 miniature buildings aboard flying bicycles with ET in a basket on the front handlebars. A ride that appeals to younger children.

Jaws®
Set amid the seaside architecture and artfully arranged lobster pots of a re-created fishing village, Captain Jake's Amity Boat Tours embark for a wholly expected watery encounter with the glistening jaws of Universal's famous 32-ft (10-m), three-ton mechanical great white shark. The steel-and-fibreglass shark moves at speeds of up to 20ft (6m) per second, with a thrust power equal to a 727 jet engine. Passengers still love it, and this is a particularly attractive corner of the park.

Jimmy Neutron's Nicktoon Blast™
A Nickelodeon children's TV animated favorite, Jimmy has leapt from small to large screen and now merits his very own theme park ride. Bucket along in the boy genius' Rocket Pod to rescue the world from evil egg-shaped Yokian aliens.

MEN IN BLACK™ Alien Attack™
An interactive chase through the streets of New York in hot pursuit of invading aliens. Terrific techno-futuristic styling, wild maneuvres and weapons that rack up your score from hero to loser.

EXPLORING

Revenge of the Mummy℠ – The Ride
The horrors and highlights of the popular Brendan Fraser film are presented here, within the frightening passages of a darkened pyramid. Super scary effects and a roller coaster race in the dark have made this a highlight.

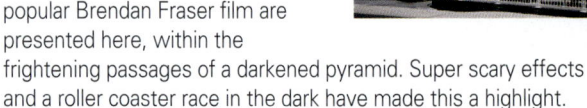

Shrek 4-D™
An adventure for the swamp-dwelling ogre and his lovely bride, Princess Fiona. Share the couple's honeymoon on 4-D "Ogrevision" complete with multi-sensory effects (including alarming pneumatic seats). The entertaining pre-show catches up non-fans on the storyline, and the show itself is a nice, fast-paced 3-D bridge between the original movie and its sequel.

The Simpsons
Stars of the small screen, then the big screen and now a theme park ride – this new attraction is set to become a classic. Head there early in the day to avoid the queues.

Terminator 2®: 3-D Battle Across Time
The world's first 3-D virtual adventure, "T2:3-D" (to aficionados) reunited the *Terminator 2* team to produce the most expensive film, frame for frame, ever made: $24 million for 12 minutes. The audience is transported into an apocalyptic world, showered with 3-D flying debris and whirlygig mini-hunter pocket gunships, and menaced by the flexi-steel pincers of the re-generating T-1,000,000. Fantastic effects: not to be missed, however long the line.

Twister… Ride It Out®
Lifted from the blockbuster movie, this multi-million dollar tornado encounter is not for the faint-hearted. Brave a five-story-high cyclone, complete with torrential rain and howling winds.

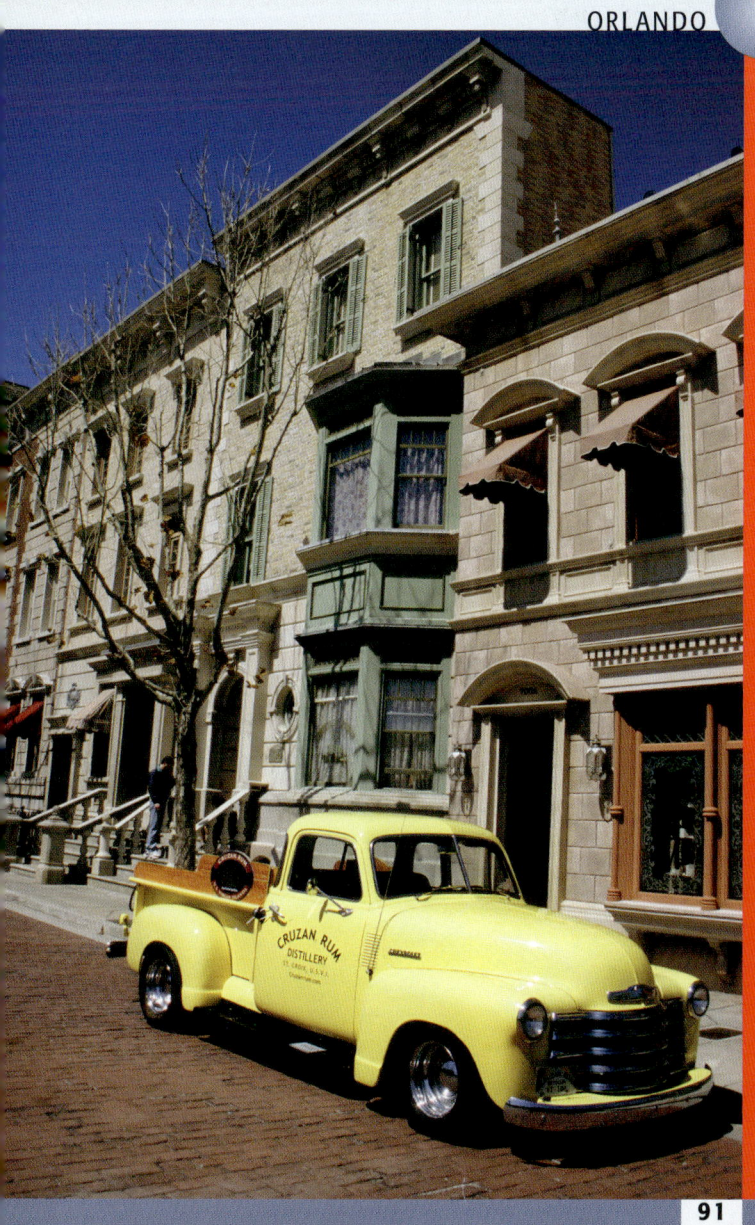

ORLANDO

EXPLORING

Universal Horror Make-Up Show
After seeing props and make-up effects from classic horror films, you enter a theater where a host and a special effects expert deliver a side-splittingly fun and funny presentation on make-up and movie tricks.

ORLANDO

Woody Woodpecker's KidZone®
A child-friendly zone of scaled down rides, adventure play areas and shows to delight the very young. Teeny thrills on Woody Woodpecker's Nuthouse Coaster, sing-a-long with the dinky dinosaurs in A Day In The Park With Barney, let off steam in Fievel's Playland or cool down amongst the water jets of the interactive Curious George Goes to Town play area.

www.universalorlando.com
✛ 16H ✉ 1000 Universal Plaza, Orlando (I-4/Exit 74B or 75A) ☎ 407/363-8000 or 1-888 322 5537 ⊙ Daily from 9am; closing times vary ✋ Very expensive. Orlando FlexTickets offer reduced rates and flexibility. Available from participating parks, 4-Park tickets provide unlimited admission to SeaWorld Orlando, Universal Studios® Escape and Wet 'nWild over 14 consecutive days. 5-Park tickets include Busch Gardens in Tampa. For further information ☎ 1-800 224 3838 🍴 Both parks offer a choice of dining options from snack stops and counter-service cafés to full-service restaurants

EXPLORING

ISLANDS OF ADVENTURE®

Universal employed the creative genius of movie director Steven Spielberg to help bring favorite comic strip characters and mythical legends to life in their second Florida theme park. Islands of Adventure® claims to be the most technologically advanced theme park in the world combining a host of hair-raising rides and boldly drawn, imaginative surroundings. Unlike its sister park, where the rides and attractions bear little relation to the stylized districts they inhabit, Islands of Adventure® has five distinctively themed "islands" linked by footbridges and water transportation from the Port of Entry. The park's highlights are listed island-by-island below.

Jurassic Park®

A lushly landscaped "island" with a familiar theme based on Spielberg's blockbuster movie. Enjoy an overview of the district from the Pteranodon Flyers aerial runway; get up close and personal with an extraordinarily lifelike "animatronic" dinosaur at the Triceratops Encounter; and prepare to ride the Jurassic Park River Adventure past a further collection of cunningly constructed prehistoric creatures with a dramatic 85-ft (26-m) waterfall plunge as a finale.

The Lost Continent®

A mythical world lost in the mists of time, the Lost Continent draws its inspiration from tales of Greek gods, Arthurian legend and the Arabian Nights. Dominating the skyline is Dueling Dragons®, an intricately designed twin roller-coaster featuring a convincing near-miss scenario; young children are relegated to the scaled-down Flying Unicorn coaster

ORLANDO

nearby. There are action-packed thrills, stunts and towering pyrotechnic effects involved in The Eighth Voyage of Sindbad® show, but the most elaborate attraction here is Poseidon's Fury® entered via a swirling water vortex hurling 17,500gal (79,545L) of water around a 42-ft (13-m) tunnel. The subsequent battle between the water god and his archrival, Zeus, employs a further 35,000gal (159,091L) of water and flame effects.

Marvel Super Hero Island
Universal's 21st-century technology has been used to create three state-of-the-art thrill rides in this primary-colored, larger-than-life land fit for super heroes. Overhead, the giant green Incredible Hulk Coaster® (it glows in the dark) blasts riders from 0 to 40 mph (65kph) in two seconds before embarking on a heartline inversion, seven roll-overs and two subterranean plunges. Across the street, guests are shot to the top of

the twin 200-ft (61-m) steel towers of Doctor Doom's Fearfall® before plummeting back down to earth. There is plenty of techno wizardry on display at the do-not-miss Amazing Adventures of Spider-Man®, which combines moving ride vehicles, spooky 3-D action and special effects in a running battle with the forces of evil out to kidnap the Statue of Liberty; and there is more special effects action in the Storm Force Accelatron® thrill ride.

Seuss Landing™
From optimum thrills to the whimsical world of Dr. Seuss, this island is especially geared towards smaller children. An assortment of suitably bizarre Seussian creatures serve as mounts on the Caro-Seuss-el, reputed to be the most elaborate carousel ever built. The One Fish Two Fish Red Fish Blue Fish ride invites guests to steer their own guppy through a series of water features guided by a special rhyme: lose the rhyme and get doused by a squirt post. If I Ran The Zoo is an interactive play area; while the best ride for accompanying adults is The Cat In The Hat™, an entertaining journey through scenes from the classic story enlivened by special effects. Or soar gently above the rides on the High in the Sky Seuss Trolley Train Ride™.

ORLANDO

Toon Lagoon
Betty Boop, Beetle Bailey and Hagar the Horrible leap out of two-dimensions and into outsize "life" on Comic Strip Lane, the main drag of Toon Lagoon. The lagoon in question is home to Me Ship, The Olive, a child-friendly play area aboard Popeye the Sailor's galleon. A short stroll away, Popeye & Bluto's Bilge-Rat Barges® shoot the rapids in a whitewater raft ride that offers an ideal way to cool down on a hot day. And for a distinctly splashy flume ride, the first ever to send passengers below water level, sit tight for Dudley Do-Right's Ripsaw Falls®.

See ▶ 93 for practical information regarding Universal's Islands of Adventure®.

WET 'N WILD
Best places to see, ▶ 50–51.

EXPLORING

HOTELS

Best Western Plaza International ($$)
Well-equipped chain hotel midway down International Drive; good rooms and suites; pool; dining; airport bus.

✉ 8738 International Drive ☎ 407/345-8195 or 1-800 780 7234; www.bestwesternplaza.com 🚌 I-Ride, Lynx #42

Best Western Universal Inn ($$)
A short drive from Universal, the single-room units feature coffeemakers, irons, hair dryers and some with refrigerators and microwaves. A free expanded continental breakfast adds to the value.

✉ 5618 Vineland Road ☎ 407/226-9119; www.bestwestern.com

Clarion Hotel Universal ($$)
Near Wet 'n Wild and tourist-friendly International Drive, the rooms are standard one-bedroom units with the added bonus of free local calls. The hotel features two restaurants, a cocktail lounge, coin laundry, heated pool, whirlpools, a flood-lit tennis court and basketball.

✉ 7299 Universal Boulevard ☎ 407/351-5009 or 1-800 445 7299; www.clarionuniversal.com

Comfort Inn International ($$)
A safe bet on I-Drive, with refrigerators, coffeemakers and, for a fee, high-speed Internet connection. If the outdoor pool's not enough to keep you fit, an off-site health club is available for a fee. Breakfast, phone calls, and transportations to Universal are free.

✉ 8134 International Drive ☎ 407/313-4000; www.choicehotels.com
🚌 I-Ride, Lynx #42

Doubletree at the Entrance to Universal Orlando ($$)
Reasonably priced rooms and suites near Universal. Amenities include dining and a late night lounge; pool; shopping arcade; kid's playground.

✉ 5780 Major Boulevard ☎ 407/351-1000 or 1-800 373 9855

ORLANDO

▼▼▼Embassy Suites International Drive South ($$$)
Well-priced two-room suites sleeping up to six people in a central location. Pools; fitness center; Family Fun Center; complimentary cooked breakfast.
✉ 8978 International Drive ☎ 407/352-1400 or 1-800 433 7275; www.embassysuites.com 🚍 I-Ride, Lynx #42

▼▼▼Fairfield Inn by Marriott ($–$$)
Close to I-Drive and dining options. Spacious, spotless rooms with high-speed internet access; outdoor heated pool, whirlpool, exercise room, video arcade and complimentary shuttle to theme parks and attractions.
✉ 7495 Canada Avenue ☎ 407/351-7000; www.marriott.com

▼▼▼Hampton Inn – International Drive Area ($$)
Small, value-priced hotel near Universal Studios and the Convention Center. All rooms have high-speed internet access, free local calls and complimentary breakfast. Other Orlando locations, including one just south of Universal Orlando.
✉ 7448 International Drive ☎ 407/313-3030 or 1-800 335 4159; http://hamptoninn.hilton.com
✉ 7110 S Kirkman Road ☎ 407/345-1112 or 1-800 335 4159

▼▼Hawthorn Suites ($–$$)
One- and two-bedroom suites with kitchen, separate living area, high-speed wireless internet access, cable TV with Nintendo. Heated pool, whirlpool, game room, exercise room and shuttle to major attractions. Second location near Universal Orlando.
✉ 6435 Westwood Boulevard ☎ 407/351-6600 or 1-800 331 5530
✉ 7601 Canada Drive ☎ 407/581-2151 or 1-866 878 4174; www.hawthorn.com

▼▼▼Homewood Suites by Hilton ($$$)
Suite hotel near Universal; one-bedroom suites with kitchens, high-speed internet, heated outdoor pool, whirlpool, exercise room and sports court.
✉ 5893 American Way ☎ 407/226-0669; www.homewood-suites.com

EXPLORING

▼▼▼▼Hyatt Regency Orlando International Airport ($$–$$$)
If you have a very early flight, this is an attractive airport hotel with direct access from the terminal and lovely spacious rooms. Facilities include restaurants, bar and pool.
✉ 9300 Airport Boulevard ☎ 407/825-1234 or 1-800 532 1496 🚌 Lynx #42

▼▼▼▼Orlando World Center Marriott ($$$)
A huge resort hotel with a choice of restaurants from fine dining to pizza; pools, 18-hole golf course, flood-lit tennis courts and health club; good children's facilities, including baby-sitting services.
✉ 8701 World Center Drive ☎ 407/239-4200 or 1-800 399 7631; www.marriottworldcenter.com 🚌 I-Ride, Lynx #42

▼▼▼▼The Peabody Orlando ($$$)
High-rise luxury hotel opposite the Convention Center, with attractive and spacious rooms and suites with a view; pool, tennis, health club; golf by arrangement. Restaurants including fine dining at Dux (➤ 103).
✉ 9801 International Drive ☎ 407/352-4000 or 1-800 732 2639; www.peabodyorlando.com 🚌 I-Ride, Lynx #42

▼▼▼▼Portofino Bay at Universal Orlando ($$$)
Luxurious Italian Riviera-themed complex with a boat to transport you to the theme parks. There are many lovely rooms; a dining area, waterfront boats, swimming pools and childminding.
✉ 5601 Universal Boulevard ☎ 407/503-1000 or 1-866 768 6658; www.loewshotels.com

▼▼▼Residence Inn by Marriott ($$)
Small-scale hotel with one- and two-bedroom suites with kitchens and high-speed internet. Heated outdoor pool, whirlpool, exercise room, sports court. Complimentary full breakfast, transportation to major attractions.
✉ 7975 Canada Avenue ☎ 407/345-0117; www.marriott.com

Staybridge Suites ($$$)
Convenient for all the sights, as well as for the shopping and dining on I-Drive. One- to three-bed units available. On-site pool and bar. Also at Lake Buena Vista.
✉ 8480 International Drive ☎ 407/352-2400 or 1-800 866 4549; www.staybridge.com 🚌 I-Ride, Lynx #42

RESTAURANTS

B-Line Diner ($$)
Fun 1950s-style diner in the Peabody Orlando hotel (Dux ➤ 103, and Peabody Orlando ➤ 100). Sandwiches, salads, pizzas and milkshakes are served at this 24-hour diner but and there is also a take-out counter.
✉ Peabody Orlando, 9801 International Drive ☎ 407/345-4570
🕐 Breakfast, lunch and dinner 🚌 I-Ride, Lynx #42

Bergamo's ($$)
This Italian restaurant serves home-made pasta, fresh seafood dishes, steaks and other hearty dishes, accompanied by singing waiters.
✉ The Mercado, 8445 International Drive ☎ 407/352-3805 🕐 Dinner only
🚌 I-Ride, Lynx #42

Café Tu Tu Tango ($)
A jumbled artist's loft-themed dining room with genuine painters daubing away on site. Order from a wide choice of multi-ethnic appetizer-size eats (tapas-style) and sample sangria.
✉ 8625 International Drive ☎ 407/248-2222 🕐 Lunch and dinner
🚌 I-Ride, Lynx #42

California Pizza Kitchen ($)
Planning a trip to the mall? This innovative pizza chain makes a great re-fueling stop. Also serves pastas, salads, sups and puds.
✉ The Florida Mall, 8001 S Orange Blossom Trail ☎ 407/854-5741
🕐 Lunch and dinner
✉ Mall at Millenia, 4200 Conroy Road ☎ 407/248-7887 🕐 Lunch and dinner

EXPLORING

Charley's Steak House ($$)
Voted one of the Top Ten Steak Houses in the US by The Knife & Fork Club of America, Charley's serves prime aged beef cooked over a wood fire in a specially built pit. There's good seafood, too.
✉ 8255 International Drive ☎ 407/363-0228; www.charleyssteakhouse.com
🕐 Dinner only 🚌 I-Ride, Lynx #42

♦♦Cedar's Restaurant ($$)
Lebanese and Mediterranean dishes are the specialty here, with good vegetarian options alongside the grilled lamb, beef, chicken and fresh seafood. The menu ranges from shish kebab and gyros to more elaborate house dishes. Good wine list.
✉ 7732 W Sand Lake Road ☎ 407/351-6000 🕐 Lunch and dinner

♦♦♦Christini's Ristorante Italiano ($$$)
Gourmet Italian restaurant serving classical cuisine with some light modern touches. One of the chef's star turns is *fettucini alla Christini* and another specialty is the 26oz (737g) veal chop. Good service from waiting staff. Smart dress code.
✉ The Marketplace, 7600 Dr Phillips Boulevard/Sand Lake Road ☎ 407/345-8770 🕐 Dinner only

♦♦♦Le Coq au Vin ($$–$$$)
This one is something of a rarity: a Central Florida French restaurant that has a long-standing reputation for producing well-prepared classics in a relaxing atmosphere. Inside a cozy renovated home.
✉ 4800 S Orange Avenue ☎ 407/851-6980 🕐 Tue–Sun lunch and dinner

♦♦♦♦Delfino Vice ($$$)
Authentic Ligurian Italian cuisine based around seafood dishes served on Versace designed tableware, with views over Orlando's interpretation of Portofino Bay. Italian minstrels complete the Mediterranean atmosphere.
✉ 6501 Universal Boulevard, Portofino Bay Hotel ☎ 407/503-1415 (reservations required) 🕐 Dinner

ORLANDO

♦♦Dexter's of Thornton Park ($$)
Just a few blocks east of downtown Orlando in trendy Thornton Park, this eclectic neighborhood meeting place is popular with young professionals and local residents. Dine inside or at the sidewalk café. Dishes include a variety of creative soups, pastas, salads and entrees.
✉ 808 East Washington Street ☎ 407/648-2777 ⏰ Lunch and dinner

♦♦♦Dux ($$$)
The Peabody Orlando's award-winning signature restaurant. Elegant décor, sophisticated New American cuisine and an excellent wine cellar are all part of the package. (Jackets for men.)
✉ Peabody Orlando, 9801 International Drive ☎ 407/345-4540
⏰ Mon–Sat, dinner only 🚌 I-Ride, Lynx #42

♦♦♦Emeril's Restaurant Orlando ($$$)
America's most popular chef brought his name and skills to this eatery at CityWalk, where a wonderful mix of Old World and Louisiana cooking meet with dishes such as oven-baked pizzas to rack of lamb, to ham crusted snapper. One of the most upscale restaurants at any theme park, anywhere.
✉ Universal CityWalk ☎ 407/224-2424 ⏰ Lunch and dinner

♦♦♦Everglades Restaurant ($$$)
Sophisticated restaurant where the atmosphere, decor and menu reflect the southern Florida wetlands. Alligator Bay chowder is a house specialty, followed by dishes such as Filet Key Largo topped with crabmeat, Blackened Red Snapper or Tenderloin of Buffalo.
✉ 9840 International Drive in the Rosen Centre Hotel ☎ 407/996-2385; www.evergladesrestaurant.com ⏰ Dinner only

♦Flippers Pizza ($)
Well-priced local pizza chain specializing in hand-tossed, made-to-order pizzas, baked pasta dishes, salads and dips.
✉ 4774 Kirkman Road ☎ 407/521-0607
✉ 6125 Westwood Boulevard ☎ 407/345-0113 ⏰ Lunch and dinner

EXPLORING

Gentry's Restaurant and Wine Bar ($$$)
Eclectic American cuisine with European accents and seasonal specialities are the hallmark of this upscale restaurant. Dark wood shutters separate comfy booths, creating a cosy atmosphere.
✉ 4120 S. Orange Avenue ☎ 407/856-5188 ◷ Mon–Sat lunch and dinner, Sun brunch

♦♦The Globe ($–$$)
If you find yourself downtown, here's a place that's hip and trendy and right across from the Orange County Historical Museum. Open very early to very late, sandwiches and salads as popular as the open air setting, and many dishes reflect clever twists on classic dishes from around the globe.
✉ 25 Wall Street Court ☎ 407/849-9904 ◷ Lunch and dinner

Hard Rock Café ($$)
An Orlando outpost for the world's largest Hard Rock Café at Universal Studios, next to the Hard Rock Live auditorium. The dining area contains the usual display of rock memorabilia including Elvis's Gibson guitar and the Beatles' 1960s suits. The menu has all-American burgers, hickory-smoked barbecue chicken, salads and the charmingly named Pig Sandwich.
✉ Universal's CityWalk® ☎ 407/351-7625 ◷ Lunch and dinner

♦♦Jimmy Buffett's Margaritaville ($$)
A casual Key West-style eatery and bar that serves up mega cheeseburgers, name-sake margaritas and a side order of Jimmy Buffett tunes.
✉ Universal's CityWalk® ☎ 407/224-2155 ◷ Lunch and dinner

♦♦Latin Quarter ($$)
Food and drink from 21 Latin American nations is served amid colorful mosaic tiles and decor that reflects native architecture. Authentic recipes feature pork, beef and chicken dishes, served with black beans, plantains, yellow rice and other traditional accompaniments. Full bar, festive music and dancing till late.
✉ Universal CityWalk® ☎ 407/224-3663 ◷ Lunch and dinner

ORLANDO

🍷🍷🍷🍷Manuel's on the 28th ($$$)
Downtown's most exclusive dining room with spectacular views from the 28th floor of the Bank of America building. Sophisticated continental-"Floribbean" cuisine. Jackets preferred.
✉ 390 N Orange Avenue ☎ 407/246-6580 🕓 Dinner only

🍷🍷🍷Ming Court ($$$)
Stylish Chinese restaurant with views over manicured Oriental gardens, mini waterfalls and koi ponds. Very good fresh seafood, and there are steaks and grills as well as skillfully prepared Chinese cuisine.
✉ 9188 International Drive ☎ 407/351-9988 🕓 Lunch and dinner 🚌 I-Ride, Lynx #42

🍷🍷Numero Uno ($)
Small and friendly Latin American restaurant with generous portion control and a hearty menu of filling staples from paella Valencia to roast pork and black beans, steaks and seafood.
✉ 2499 S Orange Avenue ☎ 407/841-3840 🕓 Lunch and dinner. Closed Sun

🍷🍷Race Rock ($$)
Motor racing memorabilia and rock music in a heaven-sent dining opportunity for boy racers. First-class pizzas, pasta, burgers and chicken wings.
✉ 8986 International Drive ☎ 407/248-9876 🕓 Lunch and dinner 🚌 I-Ride, Lunx #42

🍷🍷Ran-Getsu of Tokyo ($$$)
Authentic Japanese cuisine and an attractive location overlooking a Japanese garden and koi pond. Chefs prepare traditional sushi, sukiyaki and tempura. Entertainment at weekends.
✉ 8400 International Drive ☎ 407/345-0044 🕓 Dinner only 🚌 I-Ride, Lynx #42

EXPLORING

▼▼▼Roy's ($$–$$$)
One of Orlando's gourmet hot spots. Created in Honolulu by chef Roy Yamaguchi, the menu blends western techniques, Asian ingredients and a dash of Hawaiian inspiration to create great fusion cuisine.

✉ 7760 W Sand Lake Road ☎ 407/352-4844; www.roysrestaurant.com
🕐 Dinner only 🚌 I-Ride, Lynx #42

▼▼▼Samba Room ($$)
A Latin café with rhythm and South American–Caribbean panache. Cocktails and spiced rums, seafood, grilled meats, exotic fruits and the Bossa Nova.

✉ 7468 W Sand Lake Road ☎ 407/226-0550; www.sambaroom.net
🕐 Lunch Mon–Fri and dinner Fri–Wed 🚌 I-Ride, Lynx #42

SHOPPING

Bargain World
Huge selection of cut-price Disney, MGM and Florida souvenir T-shirts, sportswear, swimwear and beach accessories.

✉ 5454 International Drive ☎ 407/351-0900 ✉ 8520 International Drive ☎ 407/352-0214 🚌 I-Ride, Lynx #42

Florida Mall
The biggest shopping experience in Orlando, with over 250 specialty stores anchored by outposts of the Saks Fifth Avenue, Sears, J. C. Penney, Burdines and Dillard's department stores. Popular brand-name fashion boutiques include Gap, Benetton and Banana Republic. If all that shopping works up a hunger, take your pick from 30 dining options in the Food Court. Located at Sand Lake Road and the Florida Turnpike, its placement on the route to and from Orlando International Airport makes it extremely popular.

✉ 8001 S Orange Blossom Trail/US441 ☎ 407/851-6255; www.simon.com
🚌 Lynx #42

Festival Bay Mall
Over 60 specialty stores and a dozen restaurants are set around an open-air courtyard. Entertainment options include cinemas, Vans

ORLANDO

Skatepark, and the new Ron Jon Surfpark with three surf pools for beginners to pros.
✉ 5250 International Drive ☎ 407/351-7718; www.shopfestivalbaymall.com
🚌 I-Ride, Lynx #42

Grand Bohemian Gallery
Located downtown in the Grand Bohemian hotel, the gallery features work by local, national and international artists. Shop for paintings, photography, sculpture, jewellery and unique gifts.
✉ 325 S. Orange Avenue ☎ 407/581-4801; www.grandbohemiangallery.com
☎ Mon 9:30–5:30, Tue–Sat 9:30am–10pm, Sun 10–3

The Mall at Millenia
Orlando's latest shopping extravaganza boasting 150-plus fashion and specialist stores from Bang & Olufsen to Gucci via Gap, Neiman Marcus, and many eateries.
✉ 4200 Conroy Road (at I-4) ☎ 407/363-3555; www.mallatmillenia.com

Orlando Fashion Square Mall
A bit far from the tourist-beaten trail in east Orlando. Among the 165 boutiques and shops are branches of Sears, Burdines and J. C. Penney department stores.
✉ 3201 E Colonial Drive/SR50 ☎ 407/896-1131;
www.orlandofashionsquare.com

Orlando International Airport
Don't despair if you're at the airport and suddenly remember you need an extra gift for someone back home. Each of the major theme parks (Disney, Universal, SeaWorld, Kennedy Space Center) has an annex store at OIA carrying their most popular souvenirs.

Orlando Premium Outlets
This Mediterranean village is the setting for over 110 discount stores with branded names including Banana Republic, Polo Ralph Lauren, Tommy Hilfiger and Versace. Savings of 25–65 percent.
✉ 8200 Vineland Avenue ☎ 407/238-7787;
www.premiumoutlets.com/orlando 🚌 I-Ride

EXPLORING

Pointe Orlando
Upscale shopping and entertainment complex. Mega book and music stores, plus a multi-screen movie theater, restaurants and sidewalk vendors.
✉ 9101 International Drive ☎ 407/248-2838; www.pointerorlando.com
🚌 I-Ride, Lynx #42

Prime Outlets Orlando
Central Florida's largest outlet mall has two full-scale malls, annexes and the Designer Outlet Center. Bargain hunters will find discounts of 25 to 65 percent off top brand names such as Reebok, Gap, Nike and Ralph Lauren. The mall also contains Orlando's only Neiman Marcus Last Call Clearance Center.
✉ 5401 W Oakridge Road ☎ 407/351-3871; www.primeoutlets.com
🕐 Mon–Sat 10–10, Sun 10–9

Sci-Fi City
The world's largest science fiction store is bursting at the seams with books, comics, games, figurines and T-shirts galore.
✉ 6006 E Colonial Drive ☎ 407/282-2292

Sports Dominator, Inc.
Massive selection of discounted sportswear, shoes and equipment from top names including Adidas, Head and Nike, with discounts of up to 50 percent on selected items.
✉ 6464 International Drive ☎ 407/354-2100 🚌 I-Ride, Lynx #42

The Universal Studios® Store
Toy and souvenir store packed with Universal merchandise from Woody Woodpecker pyjamas to cuddly Curious Georges.
✉ Universal CityWalk®, 6000 Universal Boulevard ☎ 407/363-8000

World of Denim
Stock up on the top US brand name jeans and casual wear from Levi's, Guess?, DKNY, No Fear and Timberland among others.
✉ 7623 International Drive ☎ 407/351-5704 🚌 I-Ride, Lynx #42
✉ 5210 W Irlo Bronson Memorial Highway, Kissimmee ☎ 407/390-4561

ORLANDO

ENTERTAINMENT

ALTERNATIVE ATTRACTIONS

Fun Spot Action Park
Multi-level, action-packed family attraction with go-karting, bumper cars and boats. Fairground-style rides such as the ferris wheel. Also a massive games arcade. All good fun, if a little pricey.
✉ 5551 Del Verde Way (off International Drive) ☎ 407/363-3867
🕐 Sun–Thu 10am–11pm, Fri–Sat 10am–midnight

Magical Midway
Another I-Drive family fun zone offering the full package of extreme go-kart tracks with corkscrew turns and wacky elevations, laser tag, bumper boats and cars, plus a giant slide.
✉ Pointe Orlando, 7001 International Drive ☎ 407/370-5353 🕐 Mon–Thu 2–10, Fri–Sun 10am–midnight 🚌 I-Ride, Lynx #42

Orlando Repertory Theatre
A professional theatre for family audiences, with productions such as Seussical the Musical and Charlie and the Chocolate Factory. There are evening and matinee performances, as well as classes and camps for kids.
✉ 1001 East Princeton Street ☎ 407/896-7365; www.orlandorep.com

SkyVenture
Experience a skydiving thrill without the hassle of using a plane and a parachute as a huge blow dryer places you atop a column of air to keep you afloat like a real skydiver. Just off International Drive.
✉ 6805 Visitors Circle ☎ 407/903-1150; www.skyventureorlando.com
🕐 Daily 10:30–10

WonderWorks
A Spielberg-inspired interactive games attraction boasting 100-plus exhibits from earthquake and hurricane simulators to virtual hang-gliding and laser tag. A favorite is a design-your-own roller coaster site.
✉ Pointe Orlando, 9067 International Drive ☎ 407/351-8800 🕐 Daily 9am–midnight 🚌 I-Ride, Lynx #42

NIGHTLIFE

Backstage at the Rosen
Live bands and DJs playing hits from the '70s through to the present day at I-Drive's only nightclub without a cover charge.
✉ Clarion Plaza Hotel, 9700 International Drive ☎ 407/996-9700 ext 1684
🕐 Wed–Sat 8:30pm–2am 🚌 I-Ride, Lynx #42

Club Firestone
One of Orlando's most popular bars always throbbing with loud music; Latin, hip-hop, reggae and techno-pop disco.
✉ 578 N Orange Avenue ☎ 407/872-0066; www.clubfirestone.com
🕐 Nightly until 3am

Dragon Room
Dress sharp for this downtown club where special nights include complimentary cocktail receptions, plus DJ nights with hip-hop, R&B and pop music from the '80s to current chart-toppers.
✉ 25 W Church Street ☎ 407/843-8600; www.dragonroomorlando.com
🕐 Nightly until 3am

Friday's Front Row Sports Grill
Satellite sporting entertainment on tap, all-American menu and games room.
✉ 8126 International Drive ☎ 407/363-1414 🕐 Daily 11am–2am 🚌 I-Ride, Lynx #42

The Groove
Featuring state-of-the-art sound and lighting, DJ Club and Dance mixes plus occasional live shows. Three of the seven bars are themed "mood" rooms where guests can chat over cocktails.
✉ Universal CityWalk®, 6000 Universal Boulevard ☎ 407/363-8000
🕐 Nightly until 2am

Hard Rock Live
A huge venue for live concerts, it's adjacent to the restaurant. There's a large lobby area with a full bar if you want a quiet drink.
✉ Universal CityWalk® ☎ 407/351-5483; www.hardrock.com

ORLANDO

Peacock Room
Leaning toward upscale with live jazz, a martini bar and a DJ. Winner of several local awards for their drinks and art shows.
✉ 1321 N Mills Avenue ☎ 407/228-0048 🕐 Nightly until 2am

Pointe Orlando
After dark entertainment at a choice of restaurants, clubs and a multi-screen cinema with an IMAX 3-D theater.
✉ 9101 International Drive (at Republic Drive) ☎ 407/248-2838 🕐 Daily
🚌 I-Ride, Lynx #42

Sak Comedy Lab
Best live comedy venue in Orlando. Award-winning improvisational shows at this downtown location.
✉ 380 W Amelia Street ☎ 407/648-0001; www.sak.com 🕐 Check schedules online

Tabu
A downtown venue for clubbers who prefer a more sophisticated SoBe (that's South Beach, Miami) atmosphere. State-of-the-art sound system, sushi bar, private VIP rooms with views of the dance floor on the upper level. Sunday night is Latin night.
✉ 46 N Orange Avenue ☎ 407/648-8363; www.tabunightclub.com
🕐 Tue–Sat until 3am and Sun

Universal CityWalk®
Universal's dining and entertainment zone includes the Motown Café, CityJazz, Bob Marley – A Tribute to Freedom, the NASCAR café, Jimmy Buffet's Margaritaville and Pat O'Brien's Irish bar, as well as a Hard Rock Café and a Hard Rock Live music venue.
✉ Universal Orlando®, 1000 Universal Boulevard ☎ 407/363-8000; www.universalorlando.com 🕐 Nightly

EXPLORING

SPORTS

Bass Challenger Guide Services, Inc
Full- and half-day fishing trips with all equipment and transportation provided.
☎ 407/273-8045 or 1-800 241 5314; www.basschallenger.com ◉ Daily, by arrangement

Buena Vista Water Sports at Paradise Cove
Water-ski lessons, jet ski and competition ski boat rentals, and tube rides for groups. Reserve ahead.
✉ 13245 Lake Bryan Drive ☎ 407/239-6939; www.bvwatersports.com
◉ Daily

Grand Cypress Equestrian Center
A wide variety of lessons and programs, English and Western trail rides at this up-market hotel resort.
✉ Grand Cypress Resort, One Grand Cypress Boulevard ☎ 407/239-1938 or 1-800 835 7377; www.grandcypress.com ◉ Mon–Fri 10–6, Sat–Sun 9–5

Orlando Tennis Center
A good downtown budget option with 12 soft and 5 hard courts and good facilities.
✉ 649 W Livingstone Street ☎ 407/246-2162; www.cityoforlando.net
◉ Mon–Fri 8–9:30, Sat–Sun 8–2:30

Tiki Island Volcano Golf
Life-like dinosaurs, an erupting volcano, waterfalls and a river with flamingo paddleboats enliven two 18-hole miniature golf courses.
✉ 7460 International Drive ☎ 407/248-8180;
www.tikiislandvolcanogolf.com ☎ Daily 10am–11:30pm

Around Orlando

An all-but-invisible line divides Greater Orlando from neighboring Kissimmee. Walt Disney World® has transformed the former cattle town, bringing a welter of budget hotels and low-priced attractions along US192. Kissimmee is no beauty, but it is a useful family resort area, where the prices are fair, there are thousands of accommodation options and the entertainment is on tap.

Beyond Orlando and Kissimmee, Central Florida offers a wide choice of attractive day trips. Fast highways lead to top sightseeing destinations such as the Kennedy Space Center on the Atlantic coast and Tampa's Busch Gardens. Equally accessible are the horticultural highlights of Cypress Gardens and Bok Tower Gardens, and there are unspoilt state park preserves where hiking trails, canoe runs and wildlife-spotting provide the perfect antidote to the hurly-burly of the theme parks.

EXPLORING

BUSCH GARDENS

A popular side trip from Orlando, Busch Gardens provides a full day's family entertainment in a sprawling, African-inspired zoo-cum-theme park complex. The 10 themed areas each offer a choice of attractions and represents the perfect blend of animal shows, thrill rides and quiet nature walks. The fun water rides are very wet, and rainproof capes are on sale, but few sunbaked visitors bother. However, it is a good idea to bring a change of clothes to avoid a soggy journey back home. Opposite the Busch Gardens complex, Anheuser-Busch also have a popular 36-acre (15-ha) water park, Adventure Island (summer only).
Below is a list of highlights; see also ▶ 36–37.

Bird Gardens

Flamingos, ducks, ibis and koi fish do battle with screeching gulls for titbits in the leafy lagoon areas of the Bird Gardens. There is a walk-through aviary, an eagle exhibit, bird shows and captive koala bears. On the edge of Bird Gardens, the duelling Gwazi roller-coaster rumbles over its 7,000ft (2,134m) of wooden track.

Congo
An action-packed area at the northern extent of the park, the Congo's attractions include the hair-raising Kumba roller coaster. The slightly less dramatic Python still manages two 360° loops and a 70-ft (21-m) plunge. A drenching is guaranteed on the Congo River Rapids, and onlookers can man the Waterblasters on the bridge (25c a shot). The Ubanga-Banga Bumper Cars are located here, too; the Serengeti Express Railroad train stops at the station; and the park's magnificent Bengal tigers are incarcerated on undersized Claw Island.

Crown Colony
Here you can eat at the park's only full-service dining room, the British Colonial-themed Crown Colony Restaurant. Look in on the Anheuser-Busch brewery's ceremonial draft horses and overlook the expansive Serengeti Plain as you dine on tasty entrees. With everything from salads and sandwiches to fresh seafood platters and filet mignon, the restaurant boasts good food and the air-conditioned environment means a break from the heat.

EXPLORING

Egypt
Ruined columns, giant carved figures and hieroglyphics provide the setting for a journey into Tut's Tomb, a walk-through tour of a replica pyramid tomb as discovered by the archaeologist Howard Carter in the 1920s. The contemporary news reel footage is fun, but the jewels look a little pasty. The big ride here is the 3,983-ft (2,214-m) long, 150-ft (46-m) high Montu roller coaster, featuring a heart-stopping inverted loop of 104ft (32m). The Serengeti Express Railroad train travels across the Serengeti Plain.

AROUND ORLANDO

Land of the Dragons
A well-designed adventure playground for small children, with a friendly dragon theme. The three-story Dragon's Nest treehouse is lavishly equipped with stairs and ropeways, and there are slides, a sandpit, a carousel, watery activities and a children's theater. The Living Dragons display features monitor lizards, Komodo dragons from Indonesia and giant iguanas.

Morocco
At the entrance to the park, Morocco features attractive Moorish-style architecture and a clutch of souk-like stores selling North African craft items. Ice shows are held at the Moroccan Palace Theater and other diversions scheduled in the Marrakesh Theater.

Nairobi
First stop is Myombe Reserve: The Great Ape Domain, where the park's western lowland gorillas and chimpanzees nit-pick, snooze and occasionally stir themselves to get a better look at the humans. There are vampire bats, reptiles and snakes in Curiosity Caverns; baby birds and other residents in the Animal Nursery; a petting zoo, giant tortoises and elephants.

EXPLORING

Serengeti Plain
A 60-acre (24-ha) grassland enclosure reminiscent of the African veldt, inhabited by antelopes, giraffes, lions, rhinos and zebras. The park's Edge of Africa adventure promises a safari experience with close-up views of the animals, via a series of imaginatively designed enclosures, complete with a backing track of animal sounds and a range of evocative African smells running the olfactory gamut from camp fire to termite mound. Serengeti also boasts Rhino Rally, a rugged Land Rover Safari experience which packs thrills, spills and over 100 exotic African animals into its 8-minute journey.

Stanleyville
Just the place to cool off with two great water rides: Tanganyika Tidal Wave (which soaks onlookers as well as passengers); and Stanley Falls Log Flume. The new SheiKra roller coaster is the tallest in Florida at 200 feet (61m). There are reptile encounters at Snakes and More; the warthog and orangutan habitats; and a black spider monkey colony cavorting behind the fragrant and colorful Orchid Canyon. Guests can shop for African crafts or enjoy family entertainments at the Stanleyville Theater.

Timbuktu
At the heart of the park, Timbuktu's diversions include a semi-scary 3-D film at R. L. Stine's Haunted Lighthouse; all-singing, all-dancing perfomances at the Desert Grill; thrills aboard the Scorpion roller coaster and other fairground attractions, plus arcade games.

AROUND ORLANDO

www.buschgardens.com

☩ *25b (off map)* ✉ Busch Boulevard, Tampa (75 miles/121km west of Orlando via I-4 West and I-75 North to Fowler Avenue/Exit 54) ☎ 813/987-5082 or 1-888 800 5447 🕓 Daily 10–6 (extended summer and hols)
🍽 Refreshment stops throughout park, plus: Zagora Café (Morocco); The Oasis and Desert Grill (Timbuktu); Crown Colony Restaurant (Crown Colony); Vivi Storehouse Restaurant (Congo); Zambia Smokehouse (Stanleyville); Hospitality House (Bird Gardens) ($–$$) ✋ Very expensive. Orlando FlexTickets offer reduced rates. Available from participating parks, 5-Park tickets provide unlimited admission to Busch Gardens, as well as SeaWorld Orlando, both parks at Universal and Wet 'n Wild over 14 consecutive days. The park also offers behind-the-scenes tours for an additional charge. A guide leads groups of up to 15 people on 4–5 hour Guided Adventure Tours; 30-minute Serengeti safaris allow closer contact with the animals; and groups of 7–10 participate in feeding and training encounters on Animal Adventure Tours

Serengeti Plain transport

🚆 Crown Colony. Sky Ride cable car: Crown Colony, Stanleyville. Serengeti Express Railroad: Egypt, Congo, Stanleyville

EXPLORING

a drive
A tour around Blue Spring State Park

One of the prettiest state parks in Central Florida, Blue Spring is also famous for its winter season manatee population. They usually visit between November and March, but the park is a great day out all year round, offering walking, boating and swimming opportunites, and it is a good place to enjoy a picnic.

From Orlando, take I-4 east (direction Daytona) to Exit 114. Follow US17-92 2.5 miles (4km) south to Orange City. Blue Spring State Park is signposted off to the right at the junction with W French Avenue.

AROUND ORLANDO

Lying along the wooded banks of the St Johns River, Florida's longest natural waterway, the park's namesake artesian spring is one of the largest in the US, producing around 100 million gallons (22 million liters) of water a day. It really is blue, too. The turquoise pool at the spring head is a popular swimming hole for snorkeling, scuba-diving or just splashing around to cool off in the heat of the day.

During winter the warm spring waters, which gush forth at a constant 72°F/22°C, attract manatees from the cooler waters of the St Johns. From the waterside boardwalk there is a bird's-eye view of the manatees, and dozens of different fish and turtles swimming in the spring run; numerous waterbirds also congregate here. Canoes are available for rental and there are boat trips down the St Johns to nearby Hontoon Island State Park.

Follow the walking trail which starts near the Steamboat-era Thursby House.

Thursby House itself is perched on top of an ancient shell mound, left by Timucuan Indians. The trail leads through sand pine scrub, marshland and flatwood areas of the park.

Return to Orange City and take US17-92/I-4 back to Orlando.

Distance 60-mile (97-km) round trip
Time A 45-minute drive from Orlando. Allow at least 2 hours in the park
Start/end point Orlando
Destination Blue Spring State Park ✉ 2100 W French Avenue, Orange City ☎ 386/775-3663 🕓 Daily 8am–sunset 💲 Inexpensive
Lunch Snack concessions and cold drinks available in the park

EXPLORING

AROUND ORLANDO

CENTRAL FLORIDA ZOOLOGICAL PARK

In a way, the setting of the area's largest zoo distinguishes it from others – it seems to be carved out from the Florida wilderness. You'll exit the interstate highway to reach the zoo, where shaded, winding boardwalks and paths take you from exhibit to exhibit. The usual retinue of animals are here pacing, hanging, strutting, and sleeping in what you wish were larger or more natural enclosures. There are elephants, cheetahs, mandrills and kookaburras and, in the Herpetarium, an impressive line-up of venomous and non-venomous snakes, lizards and frogs. Elsewhere, you'll encounter pumas, llamas, sloths, monkeys, crocodiles and alligators, turtles, iguanas and the beautiful bald eagle. The zoo is about 20 miles (32km) northeast of downtown Orlando in the city of Sanford.

www.centralfloridazoo.org

✚ 28f ✉ US17–92 (south of I–4/Exit104 toward Sanford) ☎ 407/323-4450
🌐 Daily 9–5, except Thanksgiving and Christmas ✋ Moderate

CONGO RIVER GOLF & EXPLORATION CO

There is a choice of routes around this nifty mini-golf course and players are challenged to follow in the footsteps of 19th-century African explorers Henry Stanley and Dr. David Livingstone. The obstacles are somewhat less dramatic and debilitating than those encountered by our heroes, but the tropical layout is well provided with waterfalls, streams and mountainous boulders beneath the swaying palm trees. For those "too pooped to putt," there are paddle boats and a games arcade. At the second location on International Drive, go-karts add to the fun.

www.congoriver.com

✚ 28c (Kissimmee) ✉ 4777 W Irlo Bronson Highway/US192 (GM 12), Kissimmee; also at 6312 International Drive, Orlando ☎ 407/396-6900
🌐 Daily 10am–midnight ✋ Moderate

EXPLORING

CROSS CREEK

This pleasant quiet rural community is home to the Majorie Kinnan Rawlings Historic State Park and well worth a visit if traveling brings you some 60 miles (97km) to the north of Orlando. The author Majorie Kinnan Rawlings lived and worked in the tiny community for two years in the 1930s, where she bought a small homestead and settled down to learn about backwoods Cracker life. She immersed herself in the countryside, learning about every plant, shrub, tree and flower. She cooked on a wood-burning stove and washed her clothes in an iron pot. Neighbours soon warmed to her friendliness and her books reflect an intimate insight into the people and the locality. Her most famous novella was *The Yearling,* for which she won a Pulitzer Prize.

You can visit the house, preserved just as she left it, complete with ancient typewriter on the porch.

✚ *25f (off map)*

Marjorie Kinnan Rawlings Historic State Park

✉ Cross Creek (21 miles/34km southeast of Gainesville on CR 325)
☎ 352/466-3672 🕓 Daily 9–5; tours Thu–Sun at 10, 11, 1, 2, 3, 4
✋ Inexpensive

CYPRESS GARDENS ADVENTURE PARK

Best places to see, ➤ 38–39.

FANTASY OF FLIGHT

Vintage planes, each with a story to tell, help illustrate aviation history at this Central Florida aviation attraction. The first thing to notice at Fantasy of Flight is the elegant 1930s and 1940s-style art deco themed buildings, designed to capture the spirit of aviation's Golden Era. Within the twin hangars and parked out on the runways are more than 40 vintage aircraft, just a part of the world's largest private collection built up over the last quarter century by aviation enthusiast Kermit Weeks.

The earliest authentic aircraft on display here, including a

AROUND ORLANDO

Sopwith Camel, date from World War I. However, illustrating the real dawn of flight, there is a reproduction of the Wright Brothers' 1903 Kitty Hawk Flyer, a cat's-cradle of wires and wooden struts, which has actually flown – if only for a few seconds at a time. A prime Golden Era exhibit with a notable history is the 1929 Ford Tri-Motor. It flew across the US coast-to-coast in 48 hours and was later used in the making of *Indiana Jones and the Temple of Doom*.

The collection of World War II fighter planes from the US, Britain and Germany are among the museum's most popular exhibits, and visitors can test out their air combat skills in the Fightertown Flight Simulators. Another themed "immersion experience" is the History of Flight, which features walk-through dioramas. Backlot Tours take visitors behind the scenes to see the restoration workshops (weather permitting).

www.fantasyofflight.com

✚ *25b* ✉ SR559, Polk City (I-4 West to Exit 44) ☎ 863/984-3500 ⏰ Daily 10–5 💰 Expensive 🍴 Compass Rose ($–$$) ❓ Call for details of hot air balloon and biplane rides

EXPLORING

AROUND ORLANDO

GREEN MEADOWS PETTING FARM
A great treat for small children, who can find the theme park experience and crowds a bit overwhelming. Here they can scamper about safely, clamber on tractors, collect acorns for the pigs and encounter other farmyard animals on the two-hour tours. Every child can milk a cow and enjoy waggon and pony rides.

Free-ranging guineafowl, peacocks and chickens peck and preen around the attractive tree-shaded compound, which provides good protection from the hot sun, and toddlers or babies can be towed around in miniature farm trailers. Picnickers are welcome.

www.greenmeadowsfarm.com

27c ✉ 1368 S Poinciana Boulevard, Kissimmee ☎ 407/846-0770 Daily 9:30–4 (last tour) Snacks, sandwiches and cold drinks available ($) Expensive

HISTORIC BOK SANCTUARY
Dutch philanthropist and publisher Edward W. Bok created these lovely woodland gardens in the 1920s and added the coquina rock and pink and gray marble bell tower, with its world-class carillon. Its 57 bronze bells range in weight from 17 to more than 22,000 lb (10,000kg) and toll each half hour. The tower is perched on top of Iron Mountain, the highest point on the Florida peninsula, and the gently sloping 157-acre (64-ha) gardens contain thousands of flowering azaleas, camellias and magnolias beneath a canopy of trees. There are tours of the elegant 1930s house and gardens in the grounds on certain days.

www.boksanctuary.org

27a ✉ CR17-A (off Alt. 27, 3 miles north of Lake Wales) ☎ 863/676-1408 Daily 8–6 (last admission 5) Moderate Garden Restaurant ($) Daily carillon recitals at 1 and 3pm; concerts for special events

EXPLORING

KENNEDY SPACE CENTER
Best places to see,
➤ 44–45.

KISSIMMEE
Kissimmee is an attractive location for budget travelers. This is the place to find reasonably priced accommodations close to Walt Disney World® Resort, and most hotels offer a free shuttle to the Disney parks. Inexpensive family restaurants are the order of the day along US192, and there are supermarkets for self-catering holidaymakers and plenty of family attractions close by. To help visitors find their way around US192, the city has erected a number of Guide-Markers (GM) along the highway. These are used in this guide to locate the various attractions.

Kissimmee's main road stretches for miles along the US192 east–west cross route, either side of I-4. Its seamless run of local attractions and small

AROUND ORLANDO

shopping centers, chain restaurants and low-rise hotels has been nicely landscaped and made more visitor-friendly with sidewalks and pedestrian access, transportation links and even bicycle racks. The downtown district, at the junction with Orange Blossom Trail, has also been restored.

A recreated turn-of-the-century Main Street, the **Old Town Kissimmee** open-air mall, provides an entertaining mixture of shops and 18 fairground rides, including the landmark Ferris wheel. On Fridays and Saturdays a classic car parade takes place here in the evening.

One of the top rodeo events on the professional Rodeo Cowboys Association southeastern circuit, the **Silver Spurs Rodeo,** takes place at Kissimmee in February and October. It features wild bucking broncos and bulls, calf roping, steer wrestling, barrel racing, rodeo clowns and more.

✚ *28c*

Silver Spurs Rodeo

☎ For information call 407/677-6336; www.silverspursrodeo.com

Old Town Kissimmee

✉ 5770 W Irlo Bronson Memorial Highway/US192 (GM 9), Kissimmee
☎ 407/396-4888 or 1-800 843 4202; www.old-town.com ⊙ 10am–11pm
✋ Free 🍴 Fast food, snacks stalls and several restaurants ($–$$)

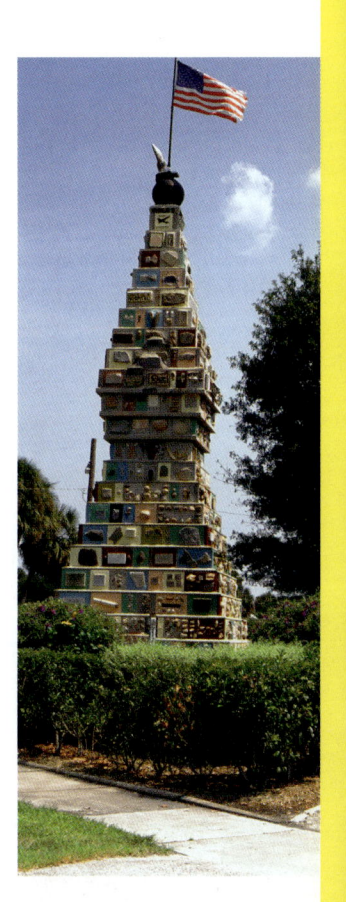

129

EXPLORING

LAKE TOHOPEKALIGA
A short step from downtown Kissimmee, Lake Toho (as it is commonly known) offers an idyllic escape from the crowds. The 13-mile (21-km) long lake covers around 22,700 acres (9,190ha), with several islands in the middle where Seminole Indians once built forts. The bass fishing is excellent, and there is great birdwatching, with more than 120 species of birds living around the lake or visiting – like the winter population of white freshwater pelicans, who fly 2,000 miles (3,225km) south to escape the chilly northern temperatures.

AROUND ORLANDO

The 30-ft (9-m) Eagle Ray excursion boat takes passengers out on the lake from Big Toho Marina. A number of outfitters offer fishing trips with a knowledgeable guide. There are also several companies offering airboat tours, such as Boggy Creek Airboat & Wildlife Safari Rides, ➤ 145.

✠ *28c*

LAKE WALES

If you'd like to experience Florida before amusement parks cropped up, visit Lake Wales. In a quiet section in the center of the state, there are still groves of oranges, grapefruit and tangerines, plus pristine lakes and Arts and Crafts cottages – and a palpable feeling of old Florida.

The **Lake Wales Museum and Cultural Center,** housed in a former railroad depot on the main street, features local history displays and railroad memorabilia. The other local attraction is Spook Hill, more correctly known as North Wales Drive. Visitors who drive to the bottom of the hill and put their vehicle in neutral at the white line will find that they appear to roll uphill.

✠ *27a*

Lake Wales Museum and Cultural Center

✉ 325 S Scenic Highway (Alt 27), Lake Wales ☎ 863/678-4209 🕓 Mon–Fri 9–5, Sat 10–4 ✋ Inexpensive

131

EXPLORING

REPTILE WORLD SERPENTARIUM
Rather off the beaten track, east of St Cloud, this no-frills serpentarium's main mission is research, and the collection and distribution of snake venoms. There are cobra and viper venom-gathering programs twice a day (at 12 and 3), and meticulous notes cover each snake display. Discover the secrets of the rattlesnake's tail, learn how to distinguish the non-venomous scarlet king snake from the poisonous eastern coral snake (same black, red and yellow coloring in subtly different proportions), and contemplate the world's largest snake species, the reticulated python and the massive green anaconda, known to snack on crocodiles in its native South America.

✚ 29c ✉ 5705 E Irlo Bronson Memorial Highway/US192, 4 miles east of St Cloud ☎ 407/892-6905 🕐 Tue–Sun 9–5:30. Closed Mon, Thanksgiving and Christmas ✋ Inexpensive

SILVER SPRINGS
Best places to see, ➤ 48–49.

SPRINGS, CENTRAL FLORIDA
One of the pure pleasures of Central Florida is lazing in the clear, cool waters of its natural springs. This is one of the few places in America where you can do this since a high limestone cap traps crystal clear 72°F (22°C) water just below the surface. The springs – most of which are safely protected within the boundaries of state parks – are just right for swimming, splashing, sunning, and paddling. In DeLand, there's great swimming and cuddly manatees at Blue Springs (➤ 120–121), and a few miles north at DeLeon Springs are the ruins of an old sugar mill and a great swimming hole. In addition to Longwood's Wekiwa Springs, Alexander

AROUND ORLANDO

Springs and Salt Springs in the Ocala National Forest are two more tranquil swimming pools and each is surrounded by great hiking trails and woodlands. Information on admission prices, directions, and hours are posted on their website.
www.dep.state.fl.us/parks
✚ Various

EXPLORING

US ASTRONAUT HALL OF FAME

Now amalgamated with the neighboring Kennedy Space Center, this is a popular stop with children, who enjoy the hands-on approach. There's lots of interactive fun here, along with space hardware exhibits from the Mercury and Gemini programs and entertaining rides such as Shuttle to Tomorrow, a flight into the future aboard a full-scale mock-up of a 120-ft (37-m) orbiter. Potential astronauts get to put themselves to the test with the G-Force Trainer, and another favorite attraction is the stomach-churning 3-D–360° flight simulator ride – which is pretty good fun to watch as well. Many of the exhibits and objects were donated by the astronauts from their personal collections.

✠ *31d* ✉ 6225 Vectorspace Boulevard/SR405, Titusville ☎ 321/269-6100 ⊙ Daily 9–5 (extended summer and hols) ✋ Moderate 🍴 Cosmic Cafe ($)

WILD WATERS

This waterpark is the place to cool off on hot summer days after visiting Silver Springs (➤ 48–49) next door. Relax under shady palms and giant oak trees or on the man-made beach. The huge, fan-shaped wave pool is surrounded by lounge chairs and sun decks. For thrill-seekers there are water slides and flume rides, including the Silver Bullet racing flume and the turbo-charged wild water Hurricane.

www.wildwaterspark.com

✠ *25f (off map)* ✉ SR40, 1 mile (1.6km) east of Ocala (72 miles/116km northwest of Orlando) ☎ 352/236-2121 ⊙ Apr–May and mid-Aug to Sep weekends 10–5, Jun to mid-Aug daily 10–6 ✋ Expensive

AROUND ORLANDO

EXPLORING

WINTER PARK

A smart northern suburb of Orlando, Winter Park boasts a brace of fine art museums, an attractive shopping district and scenic boat trips on a chain of small lakes edged by millionaires' mansions. The town was originally laid out as a genteel winter resort for wealthy New Englanders in the 1880s. Its main street, Park Avenue, is lined with boutiques and art galleries, shops selling exclusive interior design knick-knacks and chic restaurants. On Saturdays, the local Farmers' Market, on New England Avenue, is a favorite stop for fresh produce or for browsing among the colorful stalls.

✣ *28e*

Morse Museum of American Art

Pride of place goes to the gallery's world-famous collection of Tiffany glass, much of it salvaged from Laurelton Hall, Louis Comfort Tiffany's Long Island home, which burned down in 1957.

Many of Tiffany's own favorite pieces are on display, such as the glorious Rose Window. There are earthy fruit and vegetable stained-glass still lifes, others depicting magnolia blooms and elegant wisteria lampshades.

Further collections cover ceramics, furniture and metalwork, and Tiffany's contemporaries also get a look in, with glassware from René Lalique and Emile Galle, paintings by Maxfield

AROUND ORLANDO

Parrish, and contributions from Frank Lloyd Wright.
✉ 445 Park Avenue, Winter Park ☎ 407/645-5311; www.morsemuseum.org
🕐 Tue–Sat 9.30–4, Sun 1–4. Closed Mon and major hols ✋ Inexpensive

Rollins College and Cornell Fine Arts Museum

At the southern end of Park Avenue is the delightful campus of Florida's oldest college. Established in 1885, Rollins' original campus buildings were constructed in fashionable Spanish-Mediterranean style on a pretty campus overlooking Lake Virginia. Near the entrance to the campus, the Walk of Fame features more than 400 stepping stones gathered from the birthplaces and homes of famous people, from Mary, Queen of Scots and Benjamin Franklin to Buffalo Bill. There is an attractive college chapel and theater linked by a loggia, and the Cornell Fine Arts Museum houses notable collections of European Old Master paintings, 19th- and 20th-century American art, Indian objects and decorative arts.
✉ Rollins College, Holt Avenue, Winter Park ☎ 407/646-2526; www.rollins.edu/cfam 🕐 Cornell Fine Arts Museum: Tue–Sat 10–5, Sun 1–5. Closed Mon ✋ Inexpensive

Scenic Boat Tours

A chain of six little freshwater lakes around Winter Park is linked by narrow, leafy canals. The canals were once used to transport logs, but now facilitate the movement of small boats and allow scenic boat trips to putter from Lake Osceola down to Lake Virginia and up to Lake Maitland. The tours last about an hour and offer a prime view of Winter Park's most exclusive lake frontage – the grandest homes overlook Lake Maitland. Waterbirds are easy to spot and there is the occasional glimpse of an alligator.
✉ 312 E Morse Boulevard, Winter Park ☎ 407/644-4056; www.scenicboattours.com 🕐 Daily 10–4 on the hour, except Christmas ✋ Moderate

EXPLORING

HOTELS

♦♦Clarion Hotel Maingate ($$)
The 198 rooms are on two storys; pool and jacuzzi; fitness center; dining; other restaurants and shopping within walking distance.

✉ 7675 W Irlo Bronson Memorial Highway/US192, Kissimmee ☎ 407/396-4000 or 1-800 568 3352

♦♦Comfort Inn-Maingate West ($)
Located just outside Disney, this basic hotel offers a pool, free calls, and a free newspaper.

✉ 9330 West Highway 192, Kissimmee ☎ 863/424-8420 or 1-800 440 4473

♦♦Days Inn Maingate East ($–$$)
A large hotel where facilities include high-speed internet, heated outdoor pool, game room, coin laundry and playground. Complimentary transportation is available to the area's attractions.

✉ 5840 West Irlo Bronson Memorial Highway, Kissimmee ☎ 407/396-8103

♦♦Fantasy World Club Villas ($$)
Some of the two-bedroom condos come with whirlpools, all have kitchens. Four outdoor pools (two heated), whirlpool, flood-lit tennis courts, game room, playground and basketball court. Transportation to major attractions.

✉ 5005 Kyngs Heath Road, Kissimmee ☎ 407/396-8530

♦♦Howard Johnson Enchantedland Hotel ($)
A good budget option. Facilities include a heated pool, whirlpool, children's adventure club and gameroom, some of the one-bedroom units have private whirlpools. Transportation to area attractions.

✉ 4985 W Irlo Bronson Memorial Highway, Kissimmee ☎ 407/396-4343

♦♦Howard Johnson Maingate East ($$)
Reasonably spacious rooms with over half fitted with kitchens. Two pools and a playground; close to dining and shopping.

✉ 6051 W Irlo Bronson Memorial Highway/US192, Kissimmee ☎ 407/396-1748 or 1-800 446 4656

AROUND ORLANDO

⟁⟁⟁La Quinta Inn & Suites Kissimmee (Orlando Maingate) ($$)
About 3 miles (5km) from Disney and close to other attractions. There's a playground, whirlpool, heated pool, and rooms have refrigerators, microwaves and coffeemakers.
✉ 3484 Polynesian Isle Boulevard, Kissimmee ☎ 407/997-1700

⟁⟁⟁Liki Tiki Village ($–$$$)
Condos range in size at this large resort, but all have a patio or balcony. Two outdoor pools and plenty of leisure activities such as waterslide, paddleboats, bumper boats, wave pool, saunas, miniature golf, tennis courts, sports and game room. Complimentary laundry and transportation to major attractions.
✉ 17777 Bali Boulevard, Kissimmee ☎ 407/239-5000

⟁⟁Ramada Maingate West ($–$$)
Full-service resort right on Walt Disney World® Resort's doorstep. Heated outdoor and indoor pools, whirlpool, exercise room, summer recreation programs and restaurant. Free shuttle to major attractions.
✉ 7491 W Irlo Bronson Memorial Highway, Kissimmee ☎ 407/396-6000 or 1-800 669 6753

⟁⟁⟁Seralago Hotel & Suites Main Gate East ($–$$)
Large hotel with over 600 rooms and lots of amenities, including two restaurants, two heated outdoor pools, whirlpools, tennis courts, volleyball and more.
✉ 5678 W Irlo Bronson Memorial Highway, Kissimmee ☎ 407/396-4488

⟁⟁⟁Wonderland Inn ($$)
A small cottage hotel in a garden setting, it a good bed-and-breakfast option and some of the rooms have their own kitchenette. Includes a Continental breakfast and a wine/cheese hour.
✉ 3601 S Orange Blossom Trail, Kissimmee ☎ 407/847-2477 or 1-877 847 2477

RESTAURANTS

KISSIMMEE
Angels ($–$$$)
Famed locally for its seafood buffet, this restaurant serves just about every type of American food – head here if your family can't agree on one particular style of cuisine.
✉ 7300 W Irlo Bronson Memorial Highway (at the Holiday Inn) ☎ 407/397-1960 ⊕ Breakfast, lunch and dinner

Giordano's of Kissimmee ($–$$)
Always busy with visitors and locals, this family-friendly Chicago-style pizzeria also servies a selection of other favorite Italian dishes. Also at Lake Buena Vista.
✉ 7866 W Irlo Bronson Memorial Highway/US192 ☎ 407/397-0044; www.giordanos.com ✉ 12151 S Apopka-Vineland Road, Lake Buena Vista ☎ 407/239-8900 ⊕ Lunch and dinner

Key W Kool's Open Pit Grill ($$)
Nautical décor with a nod towards the Florida Keys and a steak and seafood grill menu fresh from the oakwood pit barbecue.
✉ 7725 W US192 (west of I-4) ☎ 407/396-1166 ⊕ Dinner only

Pacino's ($$)
Family-owned modern trattoria serving home-made bread and operettas, good pasta dishes, seafood and other Italian favorites.
✉ 5795 W US192 ☎ 407/396-8022 ⊕ Lunch and dinner

Smokey Bones ($$)
Real Southern barbecue. Ribs, pulled pork, beef brisket, chicken and turkey are slowly smoked over aged hickory. Grilled fish and steaks are also on the menu at this casual family dining spot.
✉ 2911 Vineland Road, Kissimmee ☎ 407/397-7102 ⊕ Lunch and dinner

LAKE WALES
Chalet Suzanne ($$$)
Award-winning restaurant in a lovely country inn, Chalet Suzanne's cozy, antique-filled dining room overlooks a small lake. The

AROUND ORLANDO

excellent American-Continental menu is short, the wine list long, the service attentive.

✉ 3800 Chalet Suzanne Drive (off CR17A, 4.5 miles (7km) north of Lake Wales) ☎ 863/676-6011 or 1-800 433 6011 ⏰ Lunch and dinner. Closed Mon

LONGWOOD
💎💎💎Enzo's on the Lake ($$–$$$)

Elegant Italian dining room with a thoroughly Mediterranean feel in a converted house overlooking Lake Fairy. Fish soup with crab and *buccatin alla Enzo* (pasta with a robust mushroom-bacon-pea sauce) are the delicious house specialties.

✉ 1130 S US17-92 ☎ 407/834-9872 ⏰ Dinner, lunch Fri only

MAITLAND
💎💎Buca di Beppo ($$)

One of the most creative Italian restaurants anywhere, with photos, artwork and memorabilia crowding every wall space. Entrees are prepared to be shared among everyone – order a plate of spaghetti and you can feed a family of four. Clever, creative, and lots of fun – although a bit far from the tourist areas.

✉ 1351 S Orlando Avenue ☎ 407/622-7663 ⏰ Dinner daily, Sunday lunch

💎💎Melting Pot ($$)

A fondue restaurant that's managed to survive in an out-of-the-way location for more than 25 years; located in Maitland, about 45 minutes from Disney. The attraction here is dishes you can prepare and cook yourself atop a small stove at your table. Follow up a combination platter with white chocolate amaretto fondue.

✉ 500 E Horatio Avenue ☎ 407/628-1134 ⏰ Dinner only

MOUNT DORA
💎💎💎Goblin Market ($$)

Inside it feels like a private library, which makes this restaurant appealing to romantics and friends who enjoy settling back to enjoy good company and conversation. Entrees are artfully presented spins on beef, pork, lamb, poultry and seafood.

✉ 330 Dora Drawdy Lane ☎ 352/735-0059 ⏰ Tue–Sun lunch and dinner

EXPLORING

♦♦Windsor Rose English Tea Room ($)
Welcoming tea room with a gift and garden shop attached. Traditional Cornish pasties, Scotch eggs and Ploughman's (bread and cheese) lunches, as well as home-made cakes and biscuits.
✉ 144 W 4th Avenue ☎ 352/735-2551 🕐 Morning coffee, lunch and tea

WINTER PARK
♦Brandywine's Deli ($)
A cute and intimate deli right on Winter Park's popular Park Avenue. People watch while dining on hearty sandwiches, diet plates, and light fare.
✉ 505 N Park Avenue ☎ 407/647-0055 🕐 All day

♦♦Briar Patch ($)
This is another Park Avenue favorite that serves fresh country-style breakfast, lunch and dinner dishes as well as delicious desserts. A nice spot to take a break from your shopping excursion.
✉ 252 N Park Avenue ☎ 407/645-4566 🕐 Breakfast, lunch and dinner

♦Bubbalou's Bodacious Bar-B-Que ($)
A local favorite for down-home BBQ sandwiches and platters. Nothing fancy, just good BBQ cooking a short drive from Winter Park's Park Avenue and the Winter Park Village shopping mall.
✉ 1471 Lee Road ☎ 407/628-1212 🕐 Lunch and dinner

♦♦Cheesecake Factory ($–$$)
Don't let the name fool you – in addition to cheesecake, there are countless types of cuisines served in a warm, fun and active atmosphere. Located at the Winter Park Village, a popular shopping and entertainment area.
✉ 520 N Orlando Avenue ☎ 407/644-4220 🕐 Lunch and dinner

♦♦♦Park Plaza Gardens ($$$)
An elegant New Orleans-style covered courtyard provides the setting for award-winning Florida cuisine. Creative dishes are served, employing the freshest local ingredients, there is a

AROUND ORLANDO

fine wine list and the service is exemplary. Sunday brunch is a local institution.

✉ 319 Park Avenue S ☎ 407/645-2475 🕓 Lunch and dinner

♦Powerhouse Café ($)
A few steps from the shopping district of Park Avenue, this little hole in the wall features organic health foods, smoothies, soups and salads in a casual, creative, student-friendly setting.

✉ 111 E Lyman Avenue ☎ 407/645-3616 🕓 Breakfast to early dinner

SHOPPING

CELEBRATION
Market Street at Celebration
Shopping with a home-town ambience in the charming boutiques, specialty shops and restaurants of this shopping district, designed by well-known architects and set around a lakeside promenade.

✉ South of Orlando off US 192 East (exit 64A from I-4) ☎ 407/566-4007; www.celebrationfl.us

COCOA BEACH
Ron Jon Surf Shop
A local institution in this lively seaside town (▶ 60). Nine acres (3.5ha) of cool surfie beach gear, sand sculptures, board or in-line skate rental and café. Open 24 hours.

✉ 4151 N Atlantic Avenue/A1A (near junction with SR520) ☎ 407/799-8888; www.ronjons.com

Merritt Square Mall
Space Coast mall with more than 80 specialty stores and restaurants and a 16-screen theater.

✉ 777 E. Merritt Island Causeway/SR520 ☎ www.merrittsquaremall.com

KISSIMMEE
Bargain World
Two Kissimmee locations for Bargain World's discounted items.

✉ 5781 W US192 (west of I-4) ☎ 407/396-7778 ✉ 7586 W US192 (east of I-4) ☎ 407/396-7199

143

EXPLORING

Old Town Kissimmee
See page 129.

Osceola Flea & Farmers Market
Sprawling 900-booth flea market (Fri–Sun) specializing in souvenirs and collectables. Also fresh local produce.
✉ 2801 E Irlo Bronson Memorial Highway/US192 ☎ 407/846-2811

Shell World
Florida's oldest and largest retailer of seashells, coral and nautical knick-knacks: 50,000 shells from around the globe from less than a dollar to valuable collectables.
✉ 4727 W Irlo Bronson Memorial Highway/US192 ☎ 407/396-9000; www.shellworld.com

MOUNT DORA
Renninger's Twin Markets
Mount Dora's antiques community is anchored by Renninger's Twin Markets, which features a side-by-side flea market and antiques market. Open each weekend.
✉ 20651 US441 east of Mount Dora, 30 minutes north of Orlando
☎ 352/383-8393

SANFORD
Flea World
America's largest weekend market under one roof (Fri–Sun): 1,700 dealer booths and thousands of bargains on souvenirs, toys, household items and unbelievable tat.
✉ US17-92 (4 miles/6km southeast of I-4/Exit 50) ☎ 407/330-1792

TITUSVILLE/MERRITT ISLAND
Space Shop
Don't blow the entire souvenir budget on Disney, the Kennedy Space Center's souvenir shop is full of unusual mementoes. Astronaut food is a favorite, plus posters and T-shirts.
✉ Kennedy Space Center, SR405 ☎ 321/449-4444

AROUND ORLANDO

WINTER PARK
Park Avenue
An attractive downtown shopping district in a north Orlando suburb. Assorted boutiques, galleries, gifts and restaurants (➤ 136).
✉ Park Avenue (at New York Avenue) ☎ 407/644-8281

Winter Park Village
A few blocks from the upscale Park Avenue, this manufactured and middle-class area is a pleasing re-creation of a Main Street shopping village; complete with sidewalk cafés, bookstores, boutiques, furniture stores and a multi-screen movie theater.
✉ 500 Orlando Avenue

ENTERTAINMENT

ALTERNATIVE ATTRACTIONS
Boggy Creek Airboat Rides
Half-hour airboat trips into the Central Florida wetlands explore 10 miles (16km) of sawgrass and natural creeks looking for wildlife. Nighttime 'gator hunts by arrangement.
✉ 2001 E Southport Rd, Kissimmee ☎ 407/344-9550; www.bcairboats.com
🕐 Daily 9–5:30 💰 Expensive

Daytona USA
Take a trip to the "World Center of Racing" visitor center at the famous Daytona Speedway. Racing memorabilia, excellent interactive displays and games, store and guided track tours.
✉ 1801 W International Speedway Boulevard/US92 (I-4/Exit 57, 50 miles (81km) east of Orlando), Daytona ☎ 386/947-6800 🕐 Apr–Oct daily 9–5

Don Garlits Museums
A popular outing for boy (or girl) racers – and their parents. There's 46,000sq ft (4,273sq m) of automotive excellence from muscle cars, hot rods and race cars to vintage Fords and a motor racing hall of fame, presented by the king of drag racing.
✉ 13700 SW 16th Avenue (55 miles (89km) north of Orlando), Ocala
☎ 352/245-8661 🕐 Daily 9–5

EXPLORING

The Ice Factory
This ice-skating center has two rinks and skating lessons. Skate rental and pro-shop, plus a children's play area, snack bar and video arcade.

✉ 2221 Partin Settlement Road, Kissimmee ☎ 407/933-4259 🕐 Public skating Mon–Fri 10–2 and Tue 5:30–7, Fri 8–11pm; Sat 1–3, 8–11; Sun 1–3

Juniper Creek Canoe Run
Great for older children. The 7-mile (11-km) canoe trail runs through the Ocala National Forest and takes around four hours. Canoes can be rented in advance.

✉ Juniper Springs Recreation Area, SR40 (22 miles/35km east of Silver Springs), Ocala National Forest ☎ 352/625-2808 or 352/625-3147 🕐 Daily 8–noon

Laneridge Winery and Vineyards
Florida's largest and award-winning winery offers interesting tours and tastings of red, white, rosé and sparkling wines.

✉ 19239 US27 North, Clermont ☎ 352/394-8627 or 1-800 768 9463; www.laneridgewinery.com 🕐 Mon–Sat 10–5, Sun 11–5

Makinson Aquatic Center
A bargain alternative to the expensive water parks, this family pool is a great place to splash around, play on the scaled-down waterslide and lounge in the sun, all for only a couple of dollars.

✉ 2204 Denn John Lane, Kissimmee ☎ 407/870-7665 🕐 Late Mar–end Sep (check schedules). Closed Mon and winter

Pirate's Cove and Pirate's Island Adventure Golf
There are two 18-hole miniature golf courses with a buccaneering theme at each of these locations.

✉ 4330 W Vine Street/US192, Kissimmee ☎ 407/396-4660
✉ 2845 Florida Plaza Boulevard, Kissimmee ☎ 407/396-7484 🕐 Daily 9am–11:30pm

Rivership Romance
Riverboat lunch and Friday and Saturday night dinner-dance cruises

AROUND ORLANDO

on Lake Monroe and St. Johns River. Popular with an older crowd.
✉ 433 N Palmetto Avenue, Sanford ☎ 407/321-5091 or 1-800 423 7401; www.rivershipromance.com 🕐 Mon–Thu 8:30–5:30, Fri–Sat 8:30–6. Sun 8:30–2

Sea Screamer
A day trip from Orlando (approx 90 mins west via I-4), Clearwater is renowned for glorious beaches and dolphin cruises. Here the 73-ft (22-m), twin-turbo Sea Screamer (the world's biggest speedboat) combines a gentle harbor cruise with a blast out into the Gulf of Mexico.
✉ Clearwater Beach Marina ☎ 727/447-7200; www.seascreamer.com
🕐 Daily at noon, 2pm, 4pm; Jun to mid-Sep also 6pm

Seminole Lake Gliderport
From a grassy airstrip in the countryside of Orlando you can take a glider (sailplane) tour with Knut Kyenslie. Flying without an engine and soaring with the birds is certainly a peaceful thrill.
✉ Highways 33 & 561, Clermont ☎ 352/394-5450; www.soarfl.com
🕐 Daily 9–5, except Mon

Warbird Adventures, Inc.
Take to the skies in T-6/ Harvard World War II fighter-trainer for an aerobatic thrill or gentle sightseeing flight.
✉ 233 N Hoagland Boulevard, Kissimmee ☎ 407/870-7366 or 1-800 386 1593; www.warbirdadventures.com 🕐 Daily 9–sunset

NIGHTLIFE
Coconuts on the Beach
The top place to party on the Space Coast, this seafood restaurant has an oceanfront deck, beachside parties and live music.
✉ 2 Minuteman Causeway, Cocoa Beach ☎ 321/784-1422; www.coconutsonthebeach.com

Heidi's Jazz Club
A hang-out for jazz lovers and jazz musicians, with live music six nights a week and featured performers on Friday and Saturday

EXPLORING

nights. Restaurant and bar menu with several German-influenced dishes.

✉ 7 N Orlando Ave, Cocoa Beach ☎ 321/783-4559; www.heidisjazzclub.com
🕐 Tue–Sun 3pm–1am

Razzles Nightclub

Dress smart for Daytona's hottest, high-energy dance club, which features a mix of hip-hop, house, trance and old skool, events and a VIP lounge.

✉ 611 Seabreeze Blvd, Daytona Beach ☎ 386/257-6236; www.razzlesnightclub.com 🕐 Nightly 10pm–3am

SPORTS

A #1 Bass Guide Service

Fully rigged bass boats and tackle for half-, full-day and nighttime fishing trips.

✉ PO Box 7544, Indian Lakes Estates, Kissimmee ☎ 352/394-3660 or 1-800 707 5463; www.a1bassguideservice.com 🕐 Daily, by arrangement

Horse World Riding Stables

Woodland trails for experienced and novice riders.

✉ 3705 S Poinciana Boulevard, Kissimmee ☎ 407/847-4343; www.horseworldstables.com 🕐 Daily from 9am

Orange Lake Country Club & Resort

Sixteen well-priced courts close to Disney; reservations are not always necessary.

✉ 8505 W Irlo Bronson Memorial Highway/US192, Kissimmee ☎ 407/239-1050; www.orangeslake.com 🕐 Daily

Walt Disney World Resort®

Walt Disney World® Resort is the apogee of the Disney phenomenon. It is a fairytale fiefdom, where litter and spoilsports are banned and Cinderella Castle pops out of the storybook and into 3-D reality. Disney's appeal is universal. It makes nonsense of age and cultural barriers uniting people from all walks of life in the pursuit of good, clean family fun and escapist fantasy. Teams of "imagineers" have resurrected everybody's favorite characters, then added the latest screen stars, state-of-the-art rides, shows and even gently educational exhibits spread over the theme parks, water parks and entertainment districts.

Some find it all too perfect, and Disney's reputation for ruthless efficiency leads to charges of blandness. However, the prime objective here is family entertainment and that, even the most grudging cynic has to admit, Disney delivers in abundance.

© Disney

149

EXPLORING

VISITING WALT DISNEY WORLD® RESORT

The cooler winter months are the most comfortable time to visit Walt Disney World® Resort, and the crowds are definitely less pressing either side of the Christmas rush (January until mid-February, and mid-September until Christmas, with the exception of the busy Thanksgiving holiday). However, expect to stand in line whenever you go, and be well prepared with loose, comfy clothing, sturdy footwear and sunblock.

Ticket options: Daily One Park/One Day admission tickets are valid for one park only on the stated day but if you plan to stay for several days, which you should do, multiple-day "Magic Your Way" base tickets offer flexibility and savings. The multi-day passes are good for one park each day your ticket is valid. For an additional $35, you can add the "park hopper" option to a ticket and have the privilege of racing from one park to the next. Another add-on is the Magic Plus Pack, which will cover admission to Disney's water parks, Pleasure Island, or the DisneyQuest® video arcade. It is best to do your homework before you arrive and check online for ticket configurations. Keep in mind that unless you purchase the additional "no expiration" option, tickets now expire 14 days after their first day of use. Guests at certain

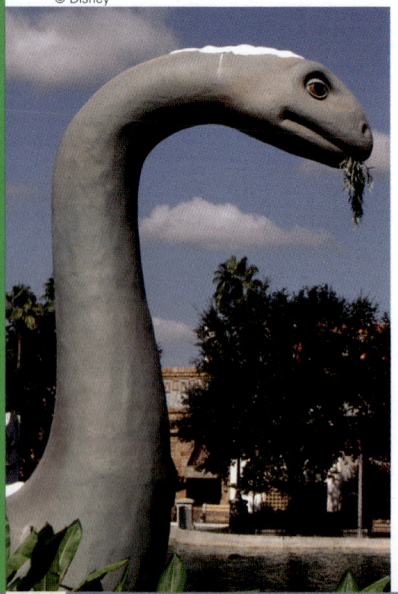

© Disney

WALT DISNEY WORLD® RESORT

properties can purchase the **Ultimate Park Hopper,** which provides admission to all Disney's WDW attractions.

FASTPASS®: Save time standing in line for the most popular rides in all four Disney theme parks with the FASTPASS® system. Simply pop your regular park ticket into the FASTPASS® machine at the attractions offering the complimentary service and you will receive a designated return time with no need to wait. The FASTPASS® allows a one-hour window from the time printed on the ticket during which you should present yourself at the FASTPASS® entrance with your ticket and sail straight through. You can only have one FASTPASS® running at any one time, i.e. you must have used (or exceeded the time allocation for) one FASTPASS® before you can collect another. Attractions offering this service are indicated on Disney maps and in this guide by the letters (FP).
What to expect: The Disney parks provide a wide range of guest facilities, from baby strollers and lockers to banking and kenneling. A limited number of wheelchairs are available, and there are special arrangements for sight- and hearing-impaired visitors. Guest relations can also help with lost and found queries, camera rentals and free battery-charging.

http://disneyworld.disney.go.com

✝ 4C ✉ Walt Disney World® Resort, Lake Buena Vista (I-4/several exits and US 192, south of Orlando) ☎ 407/824-4321 ⊙ Check current schedules ✋ Very expensive. Note that children of 10 and over qualify for adult tickets; children's tickets are for ages 3–9; under 3 free 🍴 Each park offers a wide choice of dining options open throughout the day. Reservations are advised for table service restaurants (☎ 407/939-3463) 🚌 Free shuttle bus services from many Orlando/Kissimmee hotels ❓ Details of daily parades, showtimes and night-time displays are printed in current park guides. Hotel, campground, show and ticket reservations can be made through Central Reservations (☎ 407/934-7639). Dining reservations can be made up to 60 days in advance or 180 days if you're staying at a Disney resort (☎ 407/939-3463).

EXPLORING

WALT DISNEY WORLD® RESORT

© Disney

BLIZZARD BEACH

Water sports are the specialty of Blizzard Beach, a northern ski-resort-gone-tropical water park, where the chair lifts sport sun umbrellas and the slalom course is a waterslide.

The 60-acre (24-ha) site boasts a dozen different adventure zones in the shadow of "snow-covered" Mount Gushmore. Take a chair lift up to the 60mph (97kph) Summit Plummet slide, or the slightly less dramatic Slush Gusher. Other top attractions include the Teamboat Springs white-water raft ride, inner tubing down Runoff Rapids, and the Snow Stormers flumes.

On a less frenetic note, lazy Cross Country Creek circles the park and a sandy beach borders the wave pool below Mount Gushmore. Little children can play safely at Tike's Peak; and there is shopping for essentials and souvenirs in The Village.

✚ 3A ✉ W Buena Vista Drive, Walt Disney World® Resort ☎ 407/939-7529 🕐 Daily 10–5 (extended summer and hols) ✋ Expensive (or available as option with Park Hopper Plus Pass) 🍴 Lottawatta Lodge ($–$$), Avalunch and The Warming Hut snack bars ($)

DISNEY'S ANIMAL KINGDOM® PARK

Walt Disney World® Resort's fourth full-scale theme park, Disney's Animal Kingdom® Park, focuses Disney's imagination on the natural world. The 500-acre (202-ha) site features five themed districts and has more than 200 animal species showcased in re-created naturalistic habitats. Not content with the wonders of the world about us, Disney has also gone for a fun celebration of the dinosaur era with DinoLand U.S.A®. Among all the fun, however, care has been taken to incorporate a conservationist message.

For the best chance of seeing the animals at their most active, it pays off to arrive at Disney's Animal Kingdom® as early as possible. From The Oasis entry point, head for Discovery Island® and the footbridge links to the other four districts. Then secure your first FASTPASS® (➤ 151) and check schedules for Mickey's Jammin' Jungle Parade, which tootles through the kingdom.

EXPLORING

Africa
African-styled Harambe Village is the start point for two excellent big game viewing opportunities. Kilimanjaro Safaris (FP) is Disney's Animal Kingdom®'s unmissable ride, a Jeep journey deep into the re-created African veldt inhabited by lions, cheetahs, rhinos, giraffes, wildebeest, zebras and others. The ride is brought to a rather abrupt end by a rescue mission to save the elephants from poachers, but the Pangani Forest Exploration Trail allows a closer look at some of the safari animals, notably an underwater view of the hippos, plus a lush and misty gorilla habitat. Mosey on down to Harambe Station to catch the Wildlife Express miniature train ride, which wends its way past the "backlot" animal quarters to Rafiki's Planet Watch. Here exhibits on endangered species are presented alongside picture windows viewing into the animal nursery and veterinary suite.

Asia
Exuberant rainforest-type foliage and colorful tropical flowers set the tone for the Maharaja Jungle Trek, a gentle stroll through elaborate Indian temple ruins to the tiger enclosure and exotic bird aviaries. After the trek, visit the Flights of Wonder birds of prey show, or down a cool drink in the leafy Siamang Viewing Area. Asia's action adventure is the Kali River Rapids (FP), a whitewater rafting ride that shoots beneath tunnels of overhanging bamboo, past giant boulders and cooling water jets. A new roller coaster ride, Expedition Everest, creates cutting edge excitement as it rushes forwards, backwards, up and down as you try to steer clear of the Abominable Snowman.

WALT DISNEY WORLD® RESORT

Camp Minnie-Mickey
Set slightly away from the main bustle, this is a good place for families with young children to take a break. Camp Minnie-Mickey's character greeting areas field a full team of classic Disney figures. Pocahontas and Her Forest Friends is a cute child-oriented show with live animal performers; while the Festival of the Lion King is a real crowd-pleasing spectacular for all ages, featuring acrobatic routines, fire-jugglers and stilt-walkers.

DinoLand U.S.A.®
Prehistory with a Disneyesque spin begins at the Olden Gate Bridge, a 40-ft (12-m) Brachiosaurus skeleton marking the entrance to DinoLand U.S.A.® First stop for kids is The Boneyard play area. Follow this with a visit to the Fossil Preparation Lab, where real life paleontologists undertake their research into dinosaur remains, while guests are dwarfed by the impressive collection of life-size

EXPLORING

casts taken from dinosaur skeletons in the Dinosaur Jubilee exhibition area. On the thrills front, there is rollercoaster action aboard Primeval Whirl! and the Dinosaur (FP) ride is a must, offering a time travel expedition back to the end of the dinosaur era. Dodge meteorite showers and ravening, blood-thirsty "animatronic" dinosaurs in an attempt to bring back a dear little veggie dino for posterity. For light relief, check out Finding Nemo – The Musical at the Theater in the Wild or take a four-person dino vehicle for a gentle "dino soar" with TriceraTop Spin.

Discovery Island®

At the heart of Discovery Island®, the Tree of Life is the centerpiece and symbol of the park. The trunk, branches and root system of the 145-ft (44-m) tall landmark have been carved with 325 animal images and around its vast bulk the Discovery Island® Trails meander past assorted enclosures for lemurs,

WALT DISNEY WORLD® RESORT

kangaroos, capybaras and other small- to medium-sized animals. Beneath the roots, a subterranean theater presents It's Tough to be a Bug® (FP), an entertaining 3-D look at life from a bug's perspective starring Flik and Hopper from *A Bug's Life*. (Some effects could upset small children.)

🚻 2A ✉ Osceola Parkway, Walt Disney World® Resort ☎ 407/824-4321 ⏰ Check current schedules

DISNEY'S HOLLYWOOD STUDIOS

Disney's Hollywood Studios (formerly Disney-MGM Studios) was Walt Disney World® Resort's riposte to the news that Universal Studios® was opening a rival theme park-cum-studio facility at Orlando in 1990. Disney squeezed in just ahead, opening in 1989, and have almost doubled the size of the original park, though it remains rather shorter on rides than its chief rival. However, there is plenty of Disney flair on display and constantly updated exhibits showcase new productions. Overleaf are some highlights:

🚻 3A ✉ Walt Disney World® Resort ☎ 407/824-4321

EXPLORING

Backlot Tour
After a visit to the splash tank hop aboard a tram to cruise past the Star's Parking Lot, the world's largest working wardrobe department, and the props and special effects departments. There are a couple of surprises at Catastrophe Canyon before arriving at the American Film Institute Showcase for a display of prize props and film memorabilia.

The Great Movie Ride
On Hollywood Boulevard a full-scale re-creation of Mann's Chinese Theater is the setting for this ambitious homage to movie classics. Audio-Animatronics® figures replace the stars in famous scenes.

"Honey, I Shrunk the Kids" Movie Set Adventure
An imaginative children's adventure play area featuring giant bugs, looming blades of grass and cooling water jets.

Indiana Jones® Epic Stunt Spectacular! (FP)
Check schedules with the updated show times listed in the park's free map, and catch a performance of this explosive stunt show. "Audience volunteers" get an opportunity to join in the fun.

Muppet Vision 3-D (FP)
Jim Henson's magnificent Muppets steal the show hands down. A terrific combination of big screen 70mm, 3-D film action, monster special effects and anarchic humor.

The Magic of Disney Animation
A brief but illuminating insight into the world of animation. Check out the original artworks in the animation gallery before the tour leads off through the production studios.

WALT DISNEY WORLD® RESORT

Rock 'n' Roller Coaster® Starring Aerosmith (FP)
A giant red electric guitar fronts this thrilling roller-coaster ride in the dark accompanied by a thumping soundtrack and some pretty hairy maneuvres.

Star Tours
A bone-shaking intergalatic thrill ride on a runaway space ship. Wild simulator action and dazzling special effects.

Theater of the Stars
In a setting reminiscent of the Hollywood Bowl, the 1,500-seat Theater of the Stars hosts Beauty and the Beast Live – a cute mini-musical that kids love. The Hollywood Hills Amphitheatre is the setting for Fantasmic! – and evening extravaganza featuring fireworks, action songs and a salute to Disney film and music classics. It is hugely popular so arrive early for a good seat.

The Twilight Zone Tower of Terror™ (FP)
A quiet stroll down Sunset Boulevard is soon interrupted by the shrieks of terrified passengers plummeting down the lift shaft of the spooky Hollywood Tower Hotel. Guests encounter various mysterious manifestations on the route to the top of the 199-ft (61-m) building before a series of plunges. Don't miss it.

Voyage of The Little Mermaid (FP)
Beloved of little girls the world over, Ariel gets the full theme park treatment as her story is retold with clever special effects, puppets, Audio-Animatronics, film clips and live performers.

Walt Disney: One Man's Dream
Compiled as part of Disney's 100 Years of Magic Celebration!, this look at the theme park visionary's life and achievements features objects and previously unseen film footage.

EXPLORING

DOWNTOWN DISNEY®

On the shores of Lake Buena Vista, the ever-expanding Downtown Disney® shopping, dining and entertainment complex encompasses three distinct districts: the Marketplace; Pleasure Island (➤ 175); and the rapidly expanding West Side attractions area.

Down on the lakeside, the Marketplace combines a selection of colorful boutiques and souvenir shopping outlets (➤ 182) with a handful of restaurants, including the landmark Rainforest Café (➤ 181), crowned by a volcano. During the day there are pedalboats for rental from the dock.

The neon-lit West Side boasts the state-of-the-art DisneyQuest® interactive games attraction, a 24-screen cinema complex, Virgin Records Megastore, and the Cirque du Soleil®, a 1,650-seat theater which stages glitzy, high-energy acrobatic and modern dance productions. Notable dining and entertainment venues include Orlando outposts of the House of Blues, Planet Hollywood, Wolfgang Puck Café and Gloria Estefan's Bongos Cuban Café.

✚ 5B ✉ E Buena Vista Drive, Walt Disney World® Resort ☎ 407/939-2648 🕐 Daily. Most shops stay open until 11pm or midnight; restaurants until midnight or 2am ✋ Free. Admission charged to DisneyQuest and for concerts and shows ❓ Information and reservations for Cirque du Soleil®, ☎ 407/939-7600; DisneyQuest® 407/828-4600

WALT DISNEY WORLD® RESORT

EPCOT®

Walt Disney's original plan to create a Utopian-style research community living on the Epcot® (Experimental Prototype Community of Tomorrow) site never came to fruition, but his ideas have been adapted to provide a semi-educational showcase for new technology and sciences and a window on the world around us.

Epcot®, twice the size of Magic Kingdom®, and twice as tough to navigate on foot, is divided into two parts. In the shadow of a giant silver geosphere, the **Future World** (► 162–165) pavilions house the scientific stuff, with displays focusing on transport, communications, health, energy, agriculture and oceanology. This sounds rather serious, but the Walt Disney Imagineers have added plenty of hands-on fun, rides and film shows.

The second section of the park is **World Showcase** (► 166–167), a 1.3-mile (2-km) promenade through 11 "villages," each representing the potted history, culture and architecture of a different nation.

✚ 4B ✉ Epcot® Center Drive, Walt Disney World® Resort ☎ 407/824-4321 ⊙ Check current schedules

Recommended Epcot® Restaurants

🍴 Future World: Coral Reef, The Living Seas World Showcase: Chefs de France, France; L'Originale Alfredo di Roma, Italy; Nine Dragons, China; Mitsukoshi Teppan Yaki Dining Room, Japan

❓ Make lunch or dinner reservations at Guest Relations on entering the park

161

EXPLORING

EPCOT® – FUTURE WORLD
Innoventions
Tomorrow's technology today, as top companies preview the latest developments in science and technology in an interactive environment. The two Innoventions pavilions are packed with hands-on fun from virtual tag games with Mickey and Minnie to video challenges designed to test players' problem-solving skills and knowledge of a range of science, technology and environmental subjects. Guests can build a family homepage at the Web Site Construction Zone, check out the future of the automobile, and tour the "smarthome" of tomorrow, which includes a robot dog amongst its innovations.

Journey into Imagination with Figment
A lackluster presentation narrated by Monty Python stalwart Eric Idle, who shares the billing with a perky little dragon called Figment. The rides grinds through a series of colorful scenes purporting to represent an exploration of human imagination and

© Disney

WALT DISNEY WORLD® RESORT

deposits bemused passengers into the interactive ImageWorks area to experiment with their own images. Much more fun is the hugely entertaining Honey, I Shrunk the Audience (FP) 3-D show in the movie theater.

The Land
There are three deservedly popular attractions here, starting with Living with the Land (FP). This gentle boat ride journeys through various environments explaining how plants survive, then continues into a futuristic greenhouse world where some of the fresh produce served in Walt Disney World® Resort restaurants is grown. This is quite a sight as you glide past citrus trees laden with giant 9-lb (4-kg) lemons (each capable of producing two pints of juice) and string gardens where cucumbers, eggplants and banks of lettuces grow vertically. Guests who would like a closer look at The Land's experimental greenhouses should sign up for Behind The Seeds, a behind-the-scenes guided walk tour.

Near the entrance to The Land, the Circle of Life in the Harvest

EXPLORING

© Disney

Theater is an excellent eco-conscious film show starring characters from *The Lion King*: Simba the Lion King turns Simba-the-Educator and talks Pumbaa and Timon out of polluting Africa with the Hakuna Matata Electric Disco Holiday Resort. Pretty hard-hitting stuff for Orlando.

A highly popular ride is Soarin™. Sitting under the wings of a hang glider, you're hoisted 40ft (12m) high inside a giant projection screen dome, then you take off on a virtual aerial tour of California.

The Seas with Nemo and Friends
The former Living Seas pavilion, now revamped with the popular film characters, features a 6-million-gallon salt water marine exhibit with an amazing man-made coral reef inhabited by 2,000 colorful and curious tropical fish. A ride on the clam-mobile takes you into the coral reef with views of sharks, dolphins and sea turtles. Manatees, Florida's endangered prehistoric sea cows, also feature.

Mission: SPACE
A high-tech, high thrill ride that simulates a space adventure, which launches you from a pulse-racing, adrenaline-injected lift-off to a rendezvous with weightlessness and a rough landing on Mars.

Spaceship Earth
A ride through the history of communications within the focal point of the park – a 180-ft (55-m) high aluminum geosphere. Dioramas illustrate man's progress from cave paintings to a neon journey down the Information Superhighway. Then passengers

disembark into the AT&T Global Neighborhood and its diverting assortment of hands-on games with a futuristic flavor.

Test Track
(FP) The longest and fastest ride ever created by Walt Disney Imagineers features road test automobile action. Take to the track for a tyre-squealing, three-story ascent and assorted high-speed maneuvres in the dark.

Universe of Energy
Ellen Degeneres stars with Bill Nye, the Science Guy, in a multi-screen – and occasionally humorous – presentation of the history and uses of energy. A long pre-show is just the beginning. The entire presentation lasts 45 minutes, which is a lot of valuable vacation time spent watching fake dinosaurs and hearing about an oil giant's take on fossil fuels.

© Disney

EXPLORING

EPCOT® – WORLD SHOWCASE

The American Adventure
The centerpiece of the World Showcase villages presents a 30-minute dramatized history of America by Audio-Animatronic American icons Mark Twain and Benjamin Franklin.

Canada
Feast the eyes on the CircleVision 360° *O Canada!* film and stock up on maple leaf motifs at a Rockies-style exhibit.

China
A beautiful 360° film of Chinese people and landmarks, museum-quality displays of historic objects and fabulously elaborate architecture.

France
Re-created belle époque Paris in the shadow of a miniature Eiffel Tower. Café dining, wine-tasting, waterfront artists and a French perfumerie.

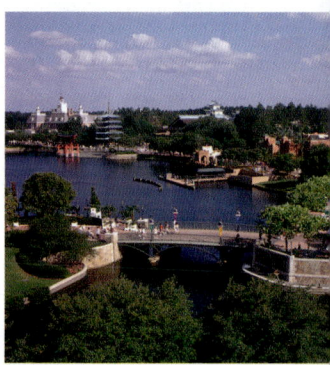

© Disney

Germany
Storybook architecture with geranium-filled window boxes, plus traditional "oompah" music piped out over the popular *biergarten*.

Italy
Venice's St. Mark's Square and the Doge's Palace recreated with scaled-down precision, along with ice creams, arias and gondolas.

Japan
Wind chimes, temple drums and a pagoda, set beside manicured gardens and koi fish ponds, give an authentic twist to this shopping and dining complex.

WALT DISNEY WORLD® RESORT

© Disney

Mexico
A huge model of a pre-Columbian pyramid and a boat ride down the River of Time attract plenty of visitors.

Morocco
An attractive Moorish souk set in narrow alleys and elegant tiled courtyards. Belly-dancing displays in the restaurant.

Norway
Malevolent trolls summon up a North Sea storm to rock the good ship *Maelstrom* (FP), a Viking longboat thrill ride in this popular Scandinavian village.

United Kingdom
Or, rather, Merrie England: a jolly knees-up with Cockney pearly kings and queens in the Rose & Crown Pub, fish and chips, warm beer and street entertainers massacring Shakespeare.

EXPLORING

MAGIC KINGDOM®

The Disney theme park that nobody wants to miss is, as a result, the most crowded, overwhelming and deserving of a second visit if you have time. Dominated by the fulsomely turreted and spired fairytale folly of Cinderella Castle, seven themed lands spread out over the 100-acre (40-ha) site, and there are 40-plus adventure attractions, dozens of daily shows, and Disney characters at every turn.

✚ 2D ✉ World Drive, Walt Disney World® Resort ☎ 407/824-4321
🌐 Check current schedules

© Disney

WALT DISNEY WORLD® RESORT

Transportation to the Magic Kingdom®
🚌 Shuttle buses pick up and drop off regularly at Transportation and Ticket Center 🚢 Ferry crosses Seven Seas Lagoon into Park; also monorail from Transportation and Ticket Center

Transportation within the Magic Kingdom®
🚆 Walt Disney World® Railroad circles the perimeter of the park, starting at main entrance, with stops at Frontierland and Mickey's Toontown Fair. Tomorrowland® Transit Authority loop ride operates within Tomorrowland®.

Cartoon Characters
✉ Disney Character Greeting Locations, highlighted on free map guides 🍴 Character dining at The Crystal Palace (Main Street); Liberty Tree Tavern (dinner only, Liberty Square); character breakfasts and lunches in Fantasyland at Cinderella's Royal Table (reservations from the City Hall information centre). For schedules and reservations: ☎ 407/939-3463

Shows and Parades
Tribute shows in the Castle Forecourt and Fantasyland several times a day. Daily, all-singing, all-dancing parade on Main Street, USA at 3pm. Check schedules for the SpectroMagic night-time parade and Wishes fireworks (nightly).

Adventureland
Lush tropical plants and eclectic colonial architecture set the scene for some of the adventures in the park. Explore the ingenious Swiss Family Treehouse, laid out amid the branches of a giant (plastic) banyan tree, and grab a pith helmet from the explorers' outfitters for a gentle rainforest Jungle Cruise (FP), which is one of the park's must-see attractions. The fast-talking skippers deliver a series of snappy one-liners on the ten-minute cruise to create an unforgettably fun adventure. Next door, the excellent Pirates of the

EXPLORING

© Disney

Caribbean adventure is a rollicking boat journey into pirate territory with noisy special effects, Audio-Animatronics buccaneers, caves full of plundered loot and a marine attack on a Caribbean island. On a less bloodthirsty note, kids will love dodging the waterspewing camels on The Magic Carpets of Aladdin, and singing totem poles and flowers join the original Tiki Birds from Disney's first-ever Audio-Animatronics show for a "hipper" version of The Enchanted Tiki Room – Under New Management.

Fantasyland

Gathered at the foot of Cinderella Castle, rides and shows are based on storybook characters designed to appeal to smaller children. Classic fairground rides include the prancing, gilded horses of Cinderella's Golden Carrousel, the whirlygig cups and saucers of the Mad Tea Party and the two-man pachyderms of Dumbo the Flying Elephant. Children can enjoy The Many Adventures of Winnie the Pooh (FP); cool off playing in the waterspouts at Ariel's Grotto; or float through the excruciatingly cute It's a Small World singing doll exhibit. Mickey's PhilharMagic (FP) is a thoroughly entertaining 3-D film where Donald Duck takes a wild ride through scenes with Aladdin, Ariel (Little Mermaid) and Simba (Lion King); 4-D sensations

170

WALT DISNEY WORLD® RESORT

include splashes of water, gusts of wind and pleasing scents.

Frontierland®
A step back in time to the Old West with stores, a shooting gallery and good thrill rides. The runaway log flume action at Splash Mountain® (FP) kicks up enough of a wave to cool off onlookers, while the Big Thunder Mountain Railroad (FP) takes passengers on a whoopin' and hollerin' roller-coaster ride. Motorized rafts potter across to Tom Sawyer Island.

Liberty Square
A genteel counterpoint to the bedlam of the neighboring Frontierland, Liberty Square has a more East Coast colonial feel and a patriotic spreading live oak, known as the Liberty Tree. Here, the Hall of Presidents presentation tackles American history in a series of lectures delivered by Audio-Animatronics US presidents. More lively by far are the undead in the Haunted Mansion (FP). This schlock-horror attraction through curtains of cobwebs, rattling bones and shrieking holograms is more rib-tickling than scary, but it's worth braving the lines. In addition, there are boat trips on the *Liberty Belle* Riverboat.

Main Street, U.S.A.
A prettified Victorian street scene, said to have been inspired by Walt Disney's childhood home in Marceline, Missouri, this broad avenue leads from the front gate up to Cinderella Castle at the

EXPLORING

hub of the park. Near the gates, in Town Square, City Hall is the main information center and depot for the horse-drawn carriages and trams that trundle up Main Street to the castle. The square also has tree-shaded areas where regular concerts are held by the Main Street Rythm Rascals. All along the route to the castle, shops sell a variety of Disney merchandise and gifts. If just arriving at the park has whetted your appetite, there's an ice-cream parlor and a bake shop.

Mickey's Toontown Fair

Home to Mickey and Minnie, this colorful corner of the park is a huge favorite with little children. Take a tour around Minnie's Country House – a veritable symphony in lilac and pink hearts and flowers with a garden to match. Mickey's Country House, next door, as you might expect, displays wardrobes full of the signature red trousers, black jackets and big boots and Pluto's dog kennel is in the garden. Children can cool off in the Donald's Boat play area, thoughtfully equipped with a bungee-soft floor and water jets; and there are pint-sized thrills to be had on The Barnstormer at Goofy's Wiseacre Farm roller-coaster.

Tomorrowland®

Dramatically updated and revamped, but top of the list here is still Space Mountain® (FP), a terrific roller-coaster ride in the dark that many rate as the top ride in the park. Tomorrowland® Indy Speedway is enduringly popular, too. Stitch's Great Escape!™ (FP) puts you on the trail of the wild, loveable alien. You join the Galactic Federation to capture Stitch, which is simply a storyline designed to introduce blackouts, weird noises and occasionally scary sensations. Further into Tomorrowland®, there are more interactive thrills aboard Buzz Lightyear's Space Ranger Spin (FP) as riders battle the evil Zurg with lasers.

On a rather gentler note, there's slapstick and belly laughs from the crew at Monsters Inc Laugh Floor. Take flight in the Astro

WALT DISNEY WORLD® RESORT

© Disney

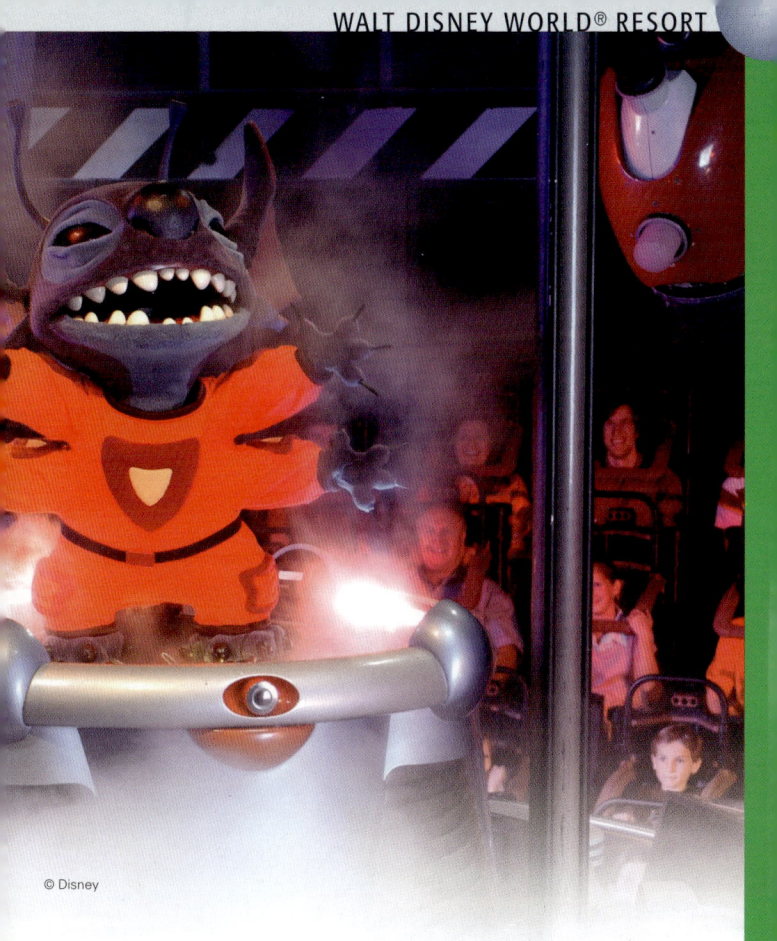

Orbiter, a mini-rocket ship ride that resembles a chunk of 1950s space cartoon hardware, but does afford a good view of the area, as does the Tomorrowland® Transit Authority, which detours into the bowels of Space Mountain® to listen to the roller-coaster passengers' screams. Debuted way back at the 1964 New York World's Fair, Walt Disney's Carousel of Progress has its share of loyal fans, but in truth this stilted Audio-Animatronics nostalgia-fest is unlikely to appeal to anybody under 60.

EXPLORING

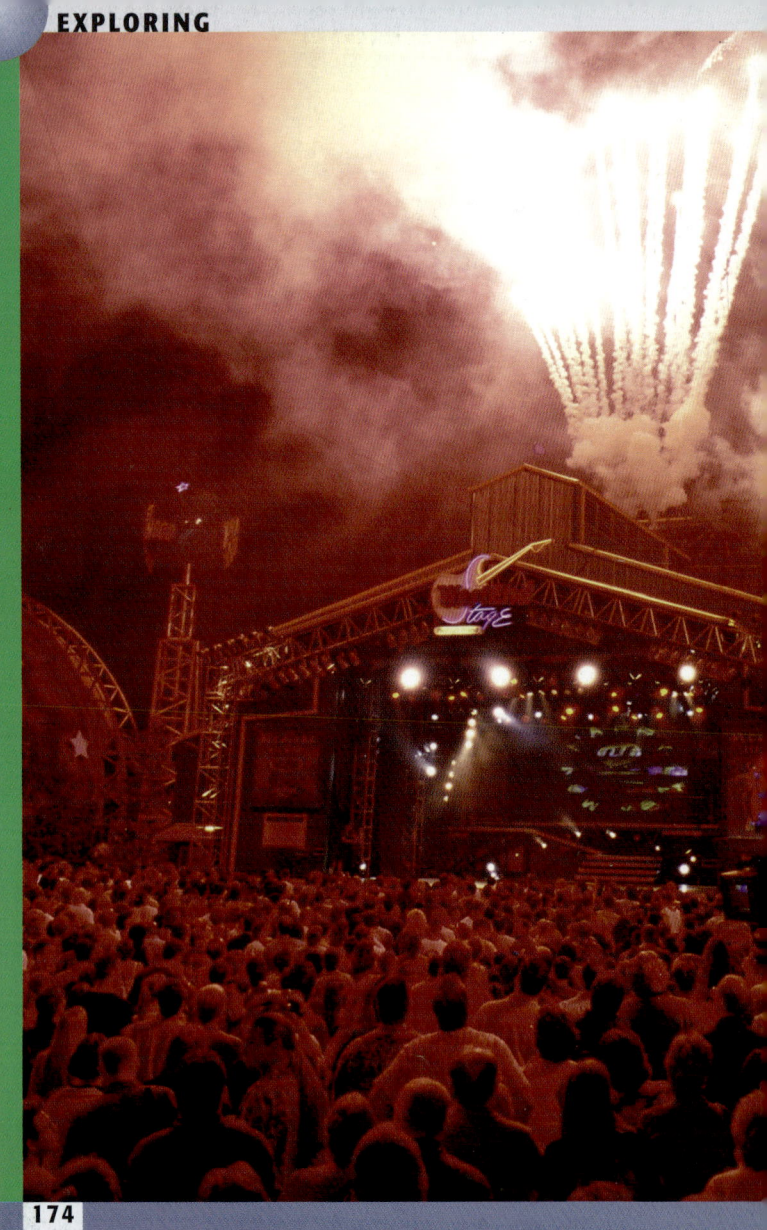

WALT DISNEY WORLD® RESORT

PLEASURE ISLAND

A 6-acre (2.5-ha) nighttime entertainment complex, Pleasure Island's one-off admission ticket entitles guests to party the night away in any or all of its eight nightclubs. There is also shopping, dining, movie theaters and dancing in the streets. Several of the shops are open during the day, when admission is free, but the real action (and paid admission) starts at 7pm and builds to a midnight New Year's Eve Street Party, complete with fireworks and a blizzard of confetti every night of the year. The revelry continues until 2am.

The night clubs run the gamut from The Comedy Warehouse, with its nightly improvisational comedy shows, to the Rock 'n' Roll Beach Club, which serves up live bands and DJs spinning hits from the 1960s up to the present day. Need to unwind after a hectic day? Then check out the music, dance and storytelling at Raglan's Road's Irish Pub. Still got energy to burn? Lava lamps and mirror balls are all the rage at 1970s-style 8 Trax; for more contemporary sounds, hit Motion, Mannequins Dance Palace or the BET Soundstage™ Club for the best in high-energy hip-hop and R&B. For something completely different, sample the interactive comedy and general weirdness on offer at the Adventurers Club.

✚ 5B ✉ E Buena Vista Drive, Walt Disney World® Resort ☎ 407/934-7781 ⏰ Daily, shops 10am–1am; clubs 7 or 8pm–2am 🍴 Light dining in the clubs ($$), also access to the Marketplace restaurants (➤ 178) ✋ Expensive (or available as option with Park Hopper Plus Pass). Additional charge for movie theaters. Occasional additional charge for special shows in specific clubs ❓ Under 18s must be accompanied by a parent; for admission to BET Soundstage™ Club and Mannequins guests must be 21 or older. All guests need a photo ID such as a passport or driving license to buy alcohol

EXPLORING

TYPHOON LAGOON
An impressive water park with an artfully shipwrecked feel, Typhoon Lagoon's showpiece is the 2.5-acre (1-ha) lagoon with surf-sized 6-ft (2-m) waves rolling onto sandy beaches every 90 seconds. Rocky Mount Mayday is landscaped with flumes and waterslides, and snorkelers can explore the 362,000-gallon salt-water coral reef environment, Shark Reef, inhabited by real tropical fish. For the biggest thrills in the park, though, check out Humunga Kowabunga, an awesome trio of 30-mph (48-kph) waterslides. The Crush 'n' Gusher water coaster ride is also highly recommended; and there is the separate Ketchakidee Creek water playground for little children.

5B ✉ Epcot® Center Drive, Walt Disney World® Resort ☎ 407/824-4321 🕐 Daily 10–5 (extended summer and hols) 🍴 Leaning Palms ($), Typhoon Tilly's ($) ✋ Expensive (or available as option with Park Hopper Plus Pass)
© Disney

WALT DISNEY WORLD® RESORT

HOTELS

Staying at Disney
A few years ago, Walt Disney World® Resort saw a lot of their guests dropping in for the day and then leaving to stay at a modestly-priced motel. To fix this, they created Value Resorts; streamlined hotels that may not have all the frills of their grand resorts, but puts guests on site. The rates are competitive with off-property hotels and offer added advantages: free parking, early admission to certain parks, and complimentary transportation to the theme parks, water parks and Downtown Disney®. Each of these resorts has a theme, a large pool, restaurant, and clean rooms. Check them out online: http://disneyworld.disney.go.com

Buena Vista Palace Resort & Spa ($$$)
Luxurious and elegant hotel rooms thoughtfully equipped with spa products ideal for footsore and weary tourists. Excellent facilities; children's programs; four restaurants and a nightclub.
✉ 1900 Buena Vista Drive ☎ 407/827-2727

Disney's All-Star Sports, Movies and Music Resorts ($$)
Three good value themed resorts; all the rooms are able to accommodate four adults; good facilities.
✉ Animal Kingdom® Park Resorts Area ☎ 407/939-5000/7000/6000; reservations 407/934-7636

Disney's BoardWalk Inn and Villas ($$$)
New England-style waterfront resort with standard rooms and one-, two- and three-bedroom studios and villas sleeping 4–12 adults. Sporting facilities; children's activities; dining and shopping.
✉ 2101 N Epcot® Resorts Boulevard ☎ 407/939-5100; reservations 407/934-7639

Disney's Port Orleans-French Quarter Resort ($$$)
Mid-range hotel with an attractive New Orleans-style setting and a choice of restaurants. A range of activities on offer include swimming, tennis courts and boating.
✉ 2201 Orleans Drive ☎ 407/934-5000; reservations 407/934-7639

EXPLORING

◆◆◆Disney's Fort Wilderness Campground ($)
Woodland camp site offering hook-up facilities and cabins that can sleep six (▶ 185).
✉ 4510 N Fort Wilderness Trail ☎ 407/824-2900; reservations 407/934-7639

◆◆◆Doubletree Club Hotel Lake Buena Vista ($$)
Vibrant colors liven up this hotel, which makes it popular with children. Facilities available include a whirlpool, exercise room, heated pool, wading pool, restaurant, gift shop, and transportation to Disney.
✉ 12490 Apopka-Vineland Road, Lake Buena Vista ☎ 407/239-4646

RESTAURANTS

◆◆◆Artist Point ($$–$$$)
Hearty cooking from the Pacific Northwest fits right in with the Wilderness Lodge décor. Salmon, Penn Cove mussels, game dishes and a notable wine list. The restaurant hosts the very popular Character Breakfast, where kids can eat while meeting their favorite characters in person.
✉ Disney's Wilderness Lodge, Magic Kingdom® Resort Area ☎ 407/939-3463 ⊙ Breakfast and dinner

◆◆◆Bahama Breeze ($$)
Created and developed in Orlando, this small chain is destined to expand with its creative and zesty Caribbean takes on chicken, fish and steak dishes. An outdoor patio with live island-style entertainment is another plus. Expect a wait.
✉ 8735 Vineland Avenue, Lake Buena Vista ☎ 407/938-9010 ✉ 8849 International Drive ☎ 407/248-2499 ⊙ Lunch and dinner

◆◆Bongos Cuban Café ($$–$$$)
Restaurant and nightclub created by Miami's disco queen, Gloria Estefan, and husband Emilio. Authentic Cuban-Latin American music and food.
✉ Downtown Disney® West Side ☎ 407/828-0999 ⊙ Lunch and dinner

WALT DISNEY WORLD® RESORT

♦♦♦California Grill ($$–$$$)
Stylish Californian cuisine with views over the Magic Kingdom®. Watch the delicious designer pizzas, oak-fired beef tenderloin and seared tuna steaks being prepared in the open-to-view kitchen.
✉ Disney's Contemporary Resort, Magic Kingdom® Resort Area ☎ 407/864-1576 ◉ Dinner only

Chefs de France ($$$)
A triumvirate of top French chefs (Bocuse, Vergé and Lenôtre) provided the creative inspiration behind this upscale restaurant in Epcot®'s World Showcase. The candles, crystal and elegance make it look and feel like the Champs Elysee. Reservations are a must.
✉ Epcot®, Epcot® Center Drive ☎ 407/939-3463 ◉ Lunch and dinner

♦♦Cinderella's Royal Table ($$–$$$)
For an unforgettable experience, make a reservation and enjoy dining inside Cinderella Castle. Yes, the Castle. Dishes include prime rib, beef pie, roast chicken, barbecue and other comfort foods. Arrive early and the kids can enjoy a Disney character breakfast or lunch.
✉ Magic Kingdom® ☎ 407/939-3463 ◉ Breakfast, lunch and dinner

♦♦♦Flying Fish Cafe ($$–$$$)
Fresh seafood is creatively prepared at this busy restaurant. Fish sculptures hang from the ceiling, and there's an open kitchen. Great food and service. Save room for the lava cake, a rich chocolate dessert, and then take a stroll on the Boardwalk.
✉ 2101 N. Epcot® Resort Boulevard ☎ 407/939-3463 ◉ Dinner only

♦♦Fulton's Crab House ($$$)
Housed in a replica turn-of-the-last-century riverboat permanently moored to the shore of Lake Buena Vista, this seafood restaurant is popular, so be prepared to have to wait for dinner. It's usually worth it for the enormous choice of expertly prepared dishes.
✉ Downtown Disney® Marketplace, 1670 E Buena Vista Drive ☎ 407/939-3463 ◉ Lunch and dinner

EXPLORING

The Garden Grill ($$)
Near the food court inside The Land pavilion at Epcot®, this table service restaurant features character meals at lunch and dinner. As you dine, you'll slowly spin past nature scenes. Oh, some of the items on your plate were grown right here.
✉ The Land, Epcot® ☎ 407/939-3463 ⓘ Lunch and dinner

The Hollywood Brown Derby ($$–$$$)
A faithful recreation of Hollywood's famous Brown Derby restaurant, featuring comfortable 1930s-style décor.
✉ Disney-MGM Studios, W Buena Vista Drive ☎ 407/939-3463 ⓘ Lunch and dinner

Jiko ($$)
The signature restaurant of Disney's elegant and intimate Animal Kingdom® Lodge, this restaurant defines its dishes as New African – traditional African dishes with influences from other cultures. Colorful décor, exemplary service and creative cuisine. Make a night of it.
✉ Animal Kingdom® Lodge, Lake Buena Vista ☎ 407/938-3000 ⓘ Dinner only

L'Originale Alfredo di Roma Ristorante ($$–$$$)
One of the stars in Epcot®'s culinary crown and very popular. Sample the namesake *fettucine alfredo*, seafood, veal dishes and Italian wines, all served to the sound of the singing waiters.
✉ World Showcase, Epcot®, Epcot® Center Drive ☎ 407/939-3463 ⓘ Lunch and dinner

Palio ($$–$$)
Fine dining restaurant where hearty Northern Italian dishes are the backbone of the menu; *osso buco* with saffron risotto, *piccata alla Milanese* and a beef fillet with polenta and shallots. The setting is taken from the Palio horse race in Siena and includes colorful flags.
✉ 1200 Epcot® Resorts Boulevard ☎ 407/939-3463 ⓘ Dinner only

WALT DISNEY WORLD® RESORT

♦♦Pebbles ($$–$$$)
Creative New American cuisine for the "casual gourmet." Delicious salads, seafood and poultry in a relaxed atmosphere. A tiki bar and outdoor patio add to the island flavor.
✉ Crossroads Shopping Center 12551 SR535 ☎ 407/827-1111 🕐 Lunch Mon–Fri, dinner daily

♦♦Portobello Yacht Club ($$–$$$)
Generous Northern Italian cooking, featuring mountains of home-made pasta, pizzas cooked in a wood-burning brick oven and daily specials with the emphasis on fresh seafood. Bustling casual atmosphere and waterfront terrace dining overlooking Lake Buena Vista.
✉ Downtown Disney® (just outside Pleasure Island), 1650 E Buena Vista Drive ☎ 407/934-8888 🕐 Lunch and dinner

Prime Time Café ($–$$)
You'll feel like you're on television in this fun '50s TV sitcom-themed restaurant located at the Disney-MGM Studios. A TV mom takes your order and serves up home-type specialties and soda fountain drinks and asks you to join the "Clean Plate Club."
✉ Disney-MGM Studios ☎ 407/939-3463 🕐 Lunch and dinner

♦♦Rainforest Café ($$–$$$)
Enormously popular jungle-themed restaurant swathed with trees and waterfalls, parrots and piña coladas. Choose from a broad menu of American favorites with a Caribbean twist. Also at Animal Kingdom®.
✉ Downtown Disney® Marketplace, 1800 E Buena Vista Drive ☎ 407/827-8500 🕐 Lunch and dinner

♦♦Restaurant Marrakesh ($$)
Enjoy Moroccan cuisine in a re-creation of a royal palace with mosaic tile work and inlaid ceilings. Belly dancers and musicians perform regularly throughout the day.
✉ Moroccan Pavilion, Epcot® ☎ 407/939-3463 🕐 Lunch and dinner

Rose and Crown ($)
If you miss your favorite pub, drop in at Epcot®'s version where Americans and Brits belly up to the bar for beers, ales and traditional English pub fare. Outside, a dining patio overlooks the lagoon.

✉ United Kingdom Pavilion, Epcot® ☎ 407/939-3463 ⏰ Lunch only

Spoodles ($–$$)
Appetizing Mediterranean menu from wood-fired thin-crust pizzas to Greek *mezes*, North African houmous, kebabs and salads. Steak and seafood also on offer.

✉ Disney's Boardwalk, Epcot® Resort Area ☎ 407/939-3463 ⏰ Breakfast and dinner

Victoria & Alberts ($$$)
For a special, but expensive, treat this intimate restaurant, within Disney's Grand Floridian Resort, is probably Disney's best. The ever-changing menu offers six courses of meticulous and delicious world-class contemporary cuisine, reflecting both American and International influences.

✉ 4401 Grand Floridian Way ☎ 407/939-3463 ⏰ Dinner only

SHOPPING

The Art of Disney
The place to find Disney posters, animation art, glossy art books and children's story books. Also at Disney-MGM Studios.

✉ Downtown Disney® Marketplace, Buena Vista Drive ☎ 407/828-3058

Crossroads at Lake Buena Vista
Small shopping and dining complex at the entrance to Walt Disney World, plus a supermarket. If you're staying at a Disney property, this is the closest option.

✉ 12521 SR535 (opposite Hotel Plaza Boulevard) ☎ 407/827-7300

Disney's Days of Christmas
It is 25 December all year round at this Christmassy store laden with yule-themed gifts and decorations. Mickey, Minnie, Winnie

WALT DISNEY WORLD® RESORT

the Pooh and other favorite Disney characters are all dressed up and ready for the festivities.
✉ Downtown Disney® Marketplace, Buena Vista Drive ☎ 407/828-3058

Downtown Disney® Marketplace
A fun place to shop and catch the breeze off the lake. Souvenirs, resortwear and World of Disney, the biggest Disney merchandise store in the world. There are also eateries and boat hire from Cap'n Jack's Marina.
✉ Buena Vista Drive ☎ 407/828-3058; www.DowntownDisney.com

Lake Buena Vista Factory Stores
Over 30 factory-direct outlet stores and a food court. Look out for 20–75 percent off retail prices from the likes of Reebok, Liz Claiborne, Lee and Wrangler jeans from the VF-Factory Outlet, and the OshKosh B'Gosh Superstore.
✉ 15591 S Apopka-Vineland Road/SR535 (2 miles/3km south of I-4/Exit 27)
☎ 407/238-9301; www.ibvfs.com

Once Upon a Toy
16,000sq ft (1,486sq m) of Disney themed merchandise plus top toy marque Hasbro of Mr Potato man fame.
✉ Downtown Disney® Marketplace, Lane Buena Vista Drive
☎ 407/934-7745

World of Disney
The world's largest Disney superstore with just about the full range of Disney merchandise from adults and children's clothing to toys, jewelry and trinkets. Kids and kitsch-crazy adults can blow the entire budget on Minnie Mouse slippers and Tigger baby-gros.
✉ Downtown Disney® Marketplace, Buena Vista Drive ☎ 407/828-3058

Wyland Galleries of Florida
Marine paintings, sculpture and prints from one of the world's leading environmental artists famous for his giant "whaling wall murals."
✉ Disney's BoardWalk, 2101 N Epcot® Resorts Boulevard ☎ 407/560-8750

EXPLORING

ENTERTAINMENT

ALTERNATIVE ATTRACTIONS
DisneyQuest®
Five floors of state-of-the-art interactive adventures and virtual reality experiences for all ages. Dodge the realistic virtual dinosaurs, design a roller-coaster and "fly" Aladdin's magic carpet.
✉ Downtown Disney® West Side ☎ 407/828-4600 🕒 Sun–Thu 11:30–11, Fri–Sat 11:30–midnight

Richard Petty Driving Experience
Ride with a pro or drive a 630hp NASCAR stock car down the backstretch at speeds of up to 145mph (234kph).
✉ Walt Disney Speedway ☎ 407/939-0130 or 1-800 237 3889 🕒 Daily 9–4

NIGHTLIFE
Cirque du Soleil® – La Nouba™
Created exclusively for Walt Disney World by the world-renowned Cirque du Soleil®, La Nouba™ is more an experience than a show. Avant-garde choreography meets Broadway spectacle and fantastical sets. There is live music, breathtaking circus skills and the requisite dose of whimsy as cast captivate audiences.
✉ Downtown Disney® West Side ☎ 407/939-7600 🕒 Tue–Sat at 6pm and 9pm

Disney's BoardWalk
Microbrewery, duelling and grand pianos and sing-alongs at Jellyrolls, the ESPN Club Sports Bar and assorted shops, vendors and activities.
✉ 2101 N Epcot® Resorts Boulevard ☎ 407/939-5100 🕒 Nightly

House of Blues
Restaurant-cum-live music venue featuring blues, R&B, jazz and country. Occasional top-name performers (check schedules).
✉ Downtown Disney® West Side ☎ 407/934-2583; www.hob.com
🕒 Sun–Mon 11–11, Tue–Wed 11–12, Thu–Sat 11–1:30am

WALT DISNEY WORLD® RESORT

Laughing Kookaburra Good Time Bar
Popular and often very crowded hotel nightclub with a surprisingly small dance floor. There is live music, contemporary chart hits, speciality cocktails and a good party atmosphere.
✉ Wyndham Palace Resort & Spa, 1900 Buena Vista Drive ☎ 407/827-3722
🕐 Nightly until 2am

Pleasure Island
See page 175.

SPORTS

Disney's Fort Wilderness
Disney's Fort Wilderness offers an enormous range of outdoor activities, from watersports to horseback-riding. There are fishing trips for largemouth bass and a children's excursion for bluegill (ages 6–12). Joggers can pound around the 2.5-mile (4-km) jogging trail. Canoes and bicycles are available for rental; sign up for a game of volleyball or basketball; or just work on a tan down at the lakeside beach. Young children also enjoy the petting zoo.
✉ Disney's Fort Wilderness Resort and Campground, N Fort Wilderness Trail, Walt Disney World Resort ☎ 407/939-7529 🕐 Daily 10–5 (extended summer and hols) 🍴 Trail's End Restaurant ($–$$) ❓ Note that some activities are for resort guests only

Water sports at Walt Disney World® Resort
Most of Walt Disney World® Resort's hotels have waterfrontage and marinas where guests can rent a variety of small sail boats, jet boats, watersprites and pedal boats. There is water-skiing from the Fort Wilderness marina, parasailing from the Contemporary Resort, and canoeing along canals from the Fort Wilderness, Caribbean Beach, Dixie Landings and Port Orleans marinas.

Index

Adventure Island 114
Adventure Land 169–170
Africa & Rafiki's Plant Watch 154
air travel 26
airboat tours 131, 145
Alexander Springs 132–133
Amazing Adventures of Spider-Man® 19, 96
American Adventure 166
Astro Orbiter 172
Around Orlando 113–148
attractions 114–137, 145–147
hotels 138–139
nightlife 147–148
restaurants 140–143
shopping 143–145
sports 148
Audubon's Center for Birds of Prey 66

Backlot Tour 158
Behind the Seeds 163
Big Thunder Mountain Railroad 171
Bird Gardens 114
Blizzard Beach 60, 153
Blue Spring State Park 60, 120–121
boat trips 48, 137, 146–147, 171, 184
Botanical Gardens 39
Bradlee-McIntyre House 66
Busch Gardens 36–37, 114–119
Buzz Lightyear's Space Ranger Spin 172

Camp Minnie-Mickey 155
Canaveral National Seashore 60
car rental 29
Central Florida Springs 60
Central Florida Zoological Park 123
CineDome 81
Cirque du Soleil® 160
climate and seasons 22
Cocoa Beach 60
Congo River Golf & Exploration Co 123
Cornell Fine Arts Museum 137
Cross Creek 124
Crown Colony 115
Cypress Gardens Adventure Park 38–39

Daytona International Speedway 71
Daytona USA 145
DeLeon Springs 132
Digistar Planetarium 81
dinner shows 19, 64, 83
DinoLand U.S.A.® 155–156
disabilities, visitors with 151
Discovery Cove 40–41
Discovery Island® 156–157
DisneyQuest® 184
Disney-MGM Studios see Disney's Hollywood Studios
Disney's Animal Kingdom® 53, 153–157
Disney's Fort Wilderness 185
Disney's Hollywood Studios 53, 157–159
Disney's Wide World of Sports® Complex 71
Doctor Doom's Fearfall® 96
dolphins, swimming with 40
Don Garlits Museum 145
Donnelly House 63
Downtown Disney 160
drives
Blue Spring State Park 120–121
Mount Dora 62–63
driving 22, 26–27, 28–29

Earthquake® 89
electricity 32
embassies and consulates 32
emergency telephone numbers 31
Epcot® 18, 53, 161–167
ET Adventure® 89

Fantasy of Flight 124–125
Fantasyland 170–171
festivals and events 24–25, 67
food and drink 12–15
alcohol 15
dinner shows 19, 64, 83
drinking water 32
soft drinks 15, 19
see also restaurants
free attractions 66–67
Frontierland 171
Fun Spot Action Park 108

Gatorland 16, 76–77
golf 11, 25, 68–69, 71, 123, 146
Great Movie Ride 158

Green Meadows Petting Farm 127
Harry P Leu Gardens 16, 42–43
Haunted Mansion 171
health 22, 23, 32
Heritage Square 78
Historic Bok Sanctuary 16, 127
"Honey, I Shrunk the Kids" Movie Set 158
Hontoon Island State Park 121
hotels
Around Orlando 138–139
Orlando 98–101
Walt Disney World® Resort 177–178

Incredible Hulk Coaster® 95
Indiana Jones® Epic Stunt Spectacular! 158
Innoventions 162
insurance 22, 23
International Drive 16
internet access 31
Islands of Adventure® 94–97

Jaws® 89
Jimmy Neutron's Nicktoon Blast™ 89
Journey into Imagination with Figment 162–163
Jurassic Park® 94

Kennedy Space Center 44–45
Kissimmee 113, 128–129
hotels 138–139
restaurants 140
shopping 143–144
Kraft Azalea Gardens 66

Lake Eola Park 66
Lake Maitland 137
Lake Tohopekaliga 130–131
Lake Wales 131, 140
Lakeridge Winery & Vineyards 66, 146
The Land 163–164
Land of the Dragons 117
Liberty Square 171
Lost Continent 94–95

The Magic of Disney Animation 158
Magic Kingdom® 19, 53, 168–173
Magical Midway 108

Main Street, U.S.A. 171–172
manatees 17, 47, 121
Manatees Rescue 84
Marjorie Kinnan Rawlings Historic State Park 124
Marvel Super Hero Island 95–96
medical treatment 23
MEN IN BLACK™ Alien Attack™ 90
Mennello Museum 78–79
Mickey's Toontown Fair 172
Mission: SPACE 164
money 30
Muppet Vision 3-D 158
Morse Museum of American Art 136–137
Mount Dora 62–63, 141–142, 144

national holidays 24
nightlife
  Around Orlando 147–148
  Orlando 110–111
  Walt Disney World® Resort 184–185

Ocala National Forest 133
opening hours 33
Orange County Regional History Center 79
Orlando 75–112
  attractions 76–97, 109
  hotels 98–101
  nightlife 110–111
  restaurants 101–106
  shopping 106–108
  sports 112
Orlando Museum of Art 80
Orlando Science Center 80–81

Pacific Point Preserve 86
passports and visas 22
personal safety 32
Pleasure Island 174–175
Pocahontas and Her Forest Friends 155
police 31
Poseidon's Fury® 95
postal services 31, 33
public transport 28–29

Reptile World Serpentarium 132
restaurants 58–59
  Around Orlando 140–43
  Orlando 101–106
  Walt Disney World® Resort 178–182
Revenge of the Mummy℠ 90
Richard Petty Driving Experience 184
Ripley's Believe It Or Not! Orlando Odditorium 82
Rock 'n' Roller Coaster® Starring Aerosmith 159
Rollins College 137
Royellou Museum 63

St. Johns River 121
Salt Springs 133
The Seas with Nemo and Friends 164
SeaWorld Orlando 46–47, 83–87
Serengeti Plain 118
Seuss Landing™ 96
Sharks Deep Dive 86
shopping 16
  Around Orlando 143–145
  Orlando 106–108
  Walt Disney World Resort 182–183
Shrek 4-D™ 90
Shuttle to Tomorrow 134
Silver Springs 48–49
Silver Spurs Rodeo 17, 24, 25, 129
The Simpsons 54, 90
SkyVenture 109
Space Mountain® 172
Spaceship Earth 164–165
Splash Mountain® 171
Spook Hill 131
sports 11, 70–71
  Around Orlando 148
  Orlando 111–112
  Walt Disney World®Resort 185
springs of Central Florida 132–133
Stanleyville 118
Star Tours 159
Stitch's Great Escape!™ 172

Tanganyika Tidal Wave 60
taxis 28
telephones 31
Terminator 2®: 3-D Battle Across Time 90
Test Track 165

Theater of the Stars 159
ticket options 29, 150–151
time differences 23
Tomorrowland® 172–173
Tomorrowland® Indy Speedway 172
Toon Lagoon 97
tourist information
  Florida offices 30
  UK offices 23
traveling to Orlando 26–27
Twilight Zone Tower of Terror 159
Twister. . .Ride It Out® 90
Typhoon Lagoon 60, 176

Universal Horror Make-Up Show 92
Universal Orlando® Resort 54–55
Universal Studios® 88–93
Universe of Energy 165
US Astronaut Hall of Fame 134

Voyage of the Little Mermaid 159

Walk of Fame 137
Walt Disney: One Man's Dream 159
Walt Disney World® Resort 10, 52–53, 149–185
  attractions 153–176, 184
  hotels 177–178
  nightlife 184–185
  restaurants 178–182
  shopping 182–183
  sports 185
  ticket options 150–151
Warbird Adventures, Inc. 147
water sports 11, 111–112, 185
Wekiwa Springs 60
West Orange Trail 66–67
Wet 'n Wild 50–51, 60
Wild Waters 60, 134
Wings of Wonder Butterfly Conservatory 39
Winter Park 136–137, 142–143, 145
WonderWorks 109
Woody Woodpecker's KidZone® 93

Zora Neale Hurston National Museum of Fine Arts 67

187

Street index

1st Street **13M**
2nd Avenue **23M**
5th Avenue **23M**
7th Street **13K**
20th Street **20J**
29th Street **19J**
Amelia Street West **20L**
Americana Boulevard **18H**
Anderson Road **23J**
Anderson Street East **22K**
Apopka-Vineland Road **15M**
Apopka Vineland Road South **6E**
Avenue of the Stars **4B**
Bachman Road **12E**
Balboa Drive **16L**
Balcombe Road **11C**
Banyan Boulevard **15G**
Bay Drive South **6F**
Bay Hill Boulevard **6F**
Beach Boulevard **24L**
Bear Island Road **2B**
Bee Line Expressway **9D**
Bennett Road **23L**
Bluford Avenue South **13L**
Bonnet Creek Road **5C**
Briercliff Drive **22K**
Bruton Boulevard **18J**
Bryn Mawr Street **20M**
Buena Vista Drive **5B**
Bumby Avenue South **22J**
Butler National Drive **24G**
Center Drive **3D**
Center Street **13M**
Central Boulevard **22K**
Central Florida Greeneway **6A**
Central Florida Parkway **11D**
Chancellor Drive **19G**
Chelsea Street **23L**
Church Street West **20K**
Circle Drive **23L**
Clarke Road **14L**
Clay Street **21M**
Club Lake Drive **5B**
Colonial Drive East **21L**
Colonial Drive West **14L**
Columbia Street **19K**
Community Drive **5B**
Conroy Road **17H**
Conroy Windermere Road **14H**
Conway Gardens Road **23J**

Conway Road South **23J**
Corrine Drive **23M**
Curry Ford Road **24K**
Darlene Drive **6D**
Deerfield Boulevard **10C**
Division Avenue South **21K**
Dixie Belle Drive **24J**
Dopey Drive **5C**
Dump Road **1D**
East-West Expressway **22K**
Edgewater Drive **20M**
Edgewood Ranch Road **15K**
Elderberry Drive **18G**
Epcot Center Drive **4C**
Epcot Resorts Boulevard **3B**
Exchange Drive **11F**
Fenton Street **6D**
Ferncreek Avenue South **22J**
Ficquette Road **2F**
Florida's Turnpike **15J**
Floridian Way **2D**
Forester Avenue **12F**
Formosa Gardens Boulevard **1A**
Fort Wilderness Trail **3D**
Frazier Avenue **17K**
Frontier Way **3D**
Gaston Foster Road **24K**
Gateway Avenue **9D**
Gatlin Avenue **21H**
General Drive **12D**
Glenridge Way **23M**
Good Homes Road **15L**
Gore Street East **22K**
Gotha Road **14K**
Granada Boulevard **6F**
Grant Street East **22J**
Greenbelt Boulevard **17K**
Hampton Avenue **22L**
Harbor Point Boulevard **16K**
Hargill Drive **23K**
Hastings Street North **17M**
Helen Avenue **21M**
Hempel Avenue **14K**
Hiawassee Road North **16L**
Hibiscus Street **23M**
Highland Avenue **21L**
Hoffner Avenue **22H**
Holden Avenue West **19H**

Hollywood Way **16G**
Honour Road **20H**
Horse Ferry Road **15J**
Hotel Plaza Boulevard **6B**
Hudson Street North **17L**
Hunter's Creek Boulevard **10A**
IInternational Drive **7C**
IIsleworth Country Club Drive **14H**
Ivey Lane South **18K**
Jason Street **21G**
Johio Shores Road **14M**
John Young Parkway North **19J**
John Young Parkway South **10C**
Jordan Avenue **12F**
Judge Road **23G**
Kaley Avenue East **22J**
Kennedy Avenue **24H**
Kilgore Road **6E**
King Street West **20M**
Kirkman Road South **17J**
Lake Ellenor Drive **20G**
Lake Hancock Road **1E**
Lake Highland Drive **21L**
Lake Jessamine Drive **20H**
Lake Margaret Drive **23J**
Lake Marsha Drive **15H**
Lakemont Avenue South **23M**
Lake Street **6C**
Lake Sue Avenue East **23M**
Lake Underhill Road **23K**
Lakeview Drive **24M**
Lakeview Street **20L**
Lake Wills Drive **7C**
Lakewood Avenue South **13L**
Lancaster Road West **21G**
Landstreet Road West **12E**
Larissa Street **9D**
Laurel Hill Drive **16M**
Laurel Street **23L**
L B McLeod Road **17J**
Lescot Lane **18K**
Lord Barclay Drive **9B**
Magazine Road **9E**
Maguire Boulevard **23L**
Maine Street **13L**
Main Street **13J**
Malcom Road **13M**
Mandarin Drive **9F**

Marcella Drive **7F**
Marks Street East **21L**
Masters Boulevard **14G**
Maury Road **20M**
Menta Street **10C**
Metrowest Boulevard **16J**
Michigan Street East **22J**
Miller Street East **21K**
Mills Avenue North **22L**
Montgomery Avenue **13L**
Moore Road **13K**
Morton Jones Road **14K**
Nebraska Street **22L**
Nela Avenue **22G**
New Hampshire Street West **20M**
Nowell Street North **17L**
Oak Ridge Road West **19G**
Old Dixie Highway **12A**
Old Winter Garden Road **16K**
Orange Avenue North **21L**
Orange Avenue South **21K**
Orange Blossom Trail North **19M**
Orange Blossom Trail South **11D**
Orange Center Boulevard **19K**
Orange Lake Boulevard **1B**
Orange-Wood Boulevard **9E**
Ordinance Road **9E**
Orlando Avenue East **13L**
Osceola Avenue South **21J**
Osceola Parkway West **2A**
Palm Parkway **6C**
Park Ridge Gotha Road **13J**
Parramore Avenue South **20K**
Par Street East **21M**
Pennsylvania Avenue South **22M**
Pepper Mill Boulevard **11C**
Perimeter Road South **8E**
Pershing Avenue **22H**
Poinsetta Avenue **20L**
Polynesian Isles Boulevard **7A**
Pomelo Drive **9F**
Powers Drive North **16L**
Premier Row **11F**
Primrose Drive North **22L**

Princetown Street West **20M**
Radebaugh Road **18G**
Raleigh Street **17K**
Raymond Street **24M**
Reams Road **3E**
Redman Street **20H**
Remote Road **9E**
Rewis Street **13M**
Ring Road **17K**
Rio Grande Avenue S **20K**
Roat Drive **15J**
Robinson Street East **21L**
Rose Boulevard **19G**
Sand Lake Road West **9F**
Seaboard Road **18M**
Sea Harbor Drive **8D**
Seminole Drive **23G**
Semoran Boulevard South **24J**
Seven Seas Drive **2D**
Shader Road **19M**
Sherberth Road **2A**
Silver Star Road **19M**
Simmons Road **23H**
Smith Bennett Road **7D**
Southland Boulevard **11F**
South Street East **21K**
Space Coast Parkway **1A**
Spring Run Avenue **16H**
Summerfield Road **24M**
Summerlin Avenue **21J**
Taft-Vineland Road **11D**
Tampa Avenue North **19K**
Tarawood Drive **14G**
Test Road **9E**
Thorpe Road **12E**
Tibet Butler Drive **4F**
Tide Water Drive **23H**
Timberleaf Boulevard **17K**
Torrey Drive **15L**
Town Center Boulevard **11B**
Town Loop Boulevard **10B**
Universal Boulevard **8F**
Vanguard Street **9F**
Vernon Street **16L**
Vineland Avenue **7C**
Vineland Road **7A**
Virginia Drive **22L**
Vista Boulevard **4C**
Wallace Drive **7F**
Washington Street West **19K**
Wells Street **19J**
Westminster Abbey Boulevard **15J**
Westmoreland Drive North **20L**
Westover Roberts Road **14J**
Westpointe Boulevard **15J**
West Wilderness Road **3D**
Westwood Boulevard **8D**
Wetherbee Road W **11C**
Whisper Lakes Boulevard **10C**
White Road **14L**
Willie Mays Parkway **18K**
Willow Park Drive **15J**
Wilmer Avenue **17L**
Winegard Road **21G**
Winter Garden-Vineland Road **5E**
Winter Park Road **22M**
Woodcrest Drive **24M**
Woodgreen Drive **16G**
World Drive **3B**

Sight locator index

This index relates to the maps on the covers. We have given map references to the main sights of interest in the book. Grid references in italics indicate sights featured on town plans. Some sights within towns may not be plotted on the maps.

Blizzard Beach **3A**
Busch Gardens **25b** *(off map)*
Central Florida Zoological Park **28f**
Congo River Golf & Exploration Co **28c** *(Kissimmee)*
Cross Creek **25f** *(off map)*
Cypress Gardens **26a**
Discovery Cove **8D**
Disney's Animal Kingdom **2A**
Disney's Hollywood Studios **3A**
Downtown Disney **5B**
Epcot **4B**
Fantasy of Flight **25b**
Gatorland **11A**
Green Meadow Petting Farm **27c**
Harry P Leu Gardens **22M**
Heritage Square **21K**
Historic Bok Sanctuary **27a**
Islands of Adventure **16G**
Kissimmee **28c**
Lake Tohopekaliga **28c**
Lake Wales **27a**
Magic Kingdom **2D**
Mennello Museum **21M**
Orange County Regional History Center **21K**
Orlando Discovery Cove **8D**
Orlando Museum of Art **21M**
Orlando Science Center **21M**
Pleasure Island **5B**
Reptile World Serpentarium **29c**
Ripley's Orlando Odditorium **8E**
SeaWorld Orlando **8D**
Silver Springs **25f** *(off map)*
Springs **Various**
Typhoon Lagoon **5B**
Universal Orlando **16H**
Universal Studios **16H**
US Astronaut Hall of Fame **31d**
Walt Disney World Resort **4C**
Wet 'n Wild **8F**
Winter Park **28e**
Wild Waters **25f** *(off map)*

189

Acknowledgements

The Automobile Association wishes to thank the following photographers, companies and picture libraries for their assistance in the preparation of this book.

Abbreviations for the picture credits are as follows – (t) top; (b) bottom; (l) left; (r) right; (c) centre; (AA) AA World Travel Library.

4l Main Street, Old Town, Kissimmee, AA/P Bennett; **4c** News Stands, Orlando, AA/P Bennett; **4r** Expedition Everest Attraction in Asia, Disney, © Disney; **5l** Winter Park golf, AA/P Bennett; **5c** Gatorland, AA/P Bennett; **6/7** Main Street, Old Town, Kissimmee, AA/P Bennett; **8/9** Oranges, AA/P Bennett; **10/11t** Space Shuttle, Kennedy Space Center, AA/P Bennett; **10ct** World of Orchids, AA/A Souter; **10cb** Orlando architecture, AA/P Bennett; **10bl** Orange Blossom Balloon, AA/P Bennett **10br** Cypress Gardens, AA/A Souter; **11c** Universal Studios®, AA/P Bennett; **11b** Rock 'n' Roller Coaster starring Aerosmith, © Disney; **12** Hamburger, AA/J A Tims; **12/13t** Seafood Platter, AA/P Bennett; **12/13b** Winter Park street café, AA/P Bennett; **13** Chef, Delray Beach, AA/J A Tims; **14** Plate of food, AA/A Souter; **14/15t** Lake Eola, AA/A Souter; **14/15b** Waitress in a diner, AA/P Bennett; **15t** City Walk, AA/P Bennett; **15b** Orange Juice, AA/P Bennett; **16c** Hard Rock Café, International Drive, AA/P Bennett; **16b** Shopper, AA/C Sawyer; **17t** Kissimmee sign, AA/P Bennett; **16/17** Manatee, SeaWorld, AA/A Souter; **18** Morocco Pavilion, Epcot®, © Disney; **19t** Orange Tree, AA/P Bennett; **19b** Medieval Times Dinner Show, AA/P Bennett **20/21** News Stands, Orlando, AA/P Bennett; **24** Fort Liberty, AA/P Bennett; **26/27** International Drive bus, AA/P Bennett; **28t** I-Drive sign, AA/P Bennett; **28b** Row of taxis, AA/P Bennett **31** Post box, AA/C Sawyer; **34/35** Expedition Everest Attraction in Asia, Disney, © Disney; **36** Pirate Ride Busch Gardens, Busch Gardens; **36/37** Busch Gardens Flume Ride, Busch Gardens; **38/39t** Cypress Gardens, AA/A Souter; **38/39b** Cypress Gardens, AA/A Souter; **40** Discovery Cove, AA/P Bennett; **40/41** Wet 'n Wild, AA/P Bennett; **42** Leu Gardens, Patio Area, Leu Gardens; **43** Rose in Leu Gardens, Leu Gardens; **44** Rocket Garden, Kennedy Space Center, AA/P Bennett; **45** Astronaut, AA/P Bennett; **46/47t** SeaWorld, AA/P Bennett; **46/47b** SeaWorld, AA/P Bennett; **47** SeaWorld sign, AA/P Bennett; **48/49** Silver Springs National Park, Alamy/David Lyons; **50/51t** Wet and Wild, AA/P Bennett; **50/51b** Wet 'n Wild, AA/P Bennett; **52** Cinderella Castle, © Disney; **52/53** Cinderella Castle at night, © Disney; **54/55t** Shrek 4D, Universal Orlando®; **54/55b** Entrance to Universal Orlando®, Universal Orlando; **56/57** Winter Park golf, AA/P Bennett; **58/59** Hard Rock Café, Universal Orlando, AA/P Bennett; **60/61** Dolphins, Discovery Cove, AA/P Bennett; **62** Lake Dora, AA/P Bennett; **62/63** Donnelly House, Mount Dora, AA/P Bennett; **64/65** Pirates Dinner Adventure Show, AA/P Bennett; **66/67** Rollins College, AA/P Bennett; **68/69** Golfer, © Disney; **70/71** Daytona Beach Track, AA/P Bennett; **72/73** Gatorland, AA/P Bennett; **75** Python, Gatorland, AA/P Bennett; **76/77** Alligators, Gatorland, AA/P Bennett; **78/79** Menello Museum, painting by Earl Cunningham, Menello Museum; **80/81t** Children at the Orlando Science Center, Orlando Science Center; **80/81b** Orlando Science Center by night, Orlando Science Center; **82** Ripley's Believe it or Not, AA/P Bennett; **82/83** Ripley's Believe it or Not, AA/P Bennett; **84** SeaWorld, AA/A Souter; **85** SeaWorld, AA/P Bennett; **86/87t** Pirate Island Show, SeaWorld, AA/P Bennett; **86/87b** Manatee pool, SeaWorld, AA/P Bennett; **88** Hollywood Diner, Universal Studios®, AA/P Bennett; **90** Hollywood Diner, AA/P Bennett; **91** Universal Studios®, AA/P Bennett; **92/93** Universal Studios®, AA/P Bennett; **93** Universal Studios®, AA/P Bennett; **94/95** Islands of Adventure®, AA/P Bennett; **95** Islands of Adventure® Logo, Universal Studios®; **96** Popeye's Galleon, Universal Studios®; **96/97** Lost Continents, Islands of Adventure®, AA/P Bennett; **113** Kissimmee Old Town, AA/P Bennett; **114/115** Hippo in water, Busch Gardens, AA/P Bennett; **116/117** Giraffe, Busch Gardens, AA/P Bennett; **118/119** Ride at Busch Gardens, Busch Gardens; **120** Manatee, AA/P Bennett; **122** Keeper with Python, Central Florida Zoo, AA/P Bennett; **123** Elephant enclosure, Central Florida Zoo, AA/P Bennett; **124** Cypress Gardens, AA/A Souter; **126/127** Bok Tower Gardens, AA/P Bennett; **128** Kissimmee Chain o Lakes, AA/P Bennett; **129** Kissimmee monument to the United States of America, AA/P Bennett; **130/131** Lake Tohopekaliga, Alamy/Rough Guides; **132** Wekiwa Springs, AA/P Bennett; **133** Wekiwa Springs State Park, AA/P Bennett; **134** Kennedy Space Center, AA/A Souter; **135** Water Mania, Kissimmee, AA/P Bennett; **136** Winter Park, AA/P Bennett; **149** "Lights, Motor, Action" Extreme Stunt Show, © Disney; **150** "Gertie" at Echo lake in Disney-MGM Studios, © Disney; **152/153** Slush Gusher, © Disney; **154/155** Animals Carved in the Tree of Life, © Disney; **156/157** Tree of Life Attraction, © Disney; **160/161** World of Disney merchandise store, © Disney; **162/163** Mission: SPACE, © Disney; **164** Spaceship Earth, © Disney; **164/165** Japan Pavilion, Epcot®, © Disney; **166/167** Epcot® World Showcase Aerial View, © Disney; **167** Italy Pavilion, © Disney; **168/169** Wishes Fireworks Show, © Disney; **170** The Jungle Cruise, © Disney; **170/171** Magic Carpets of Aladdin, © Disney; **172/173** Stitch's Great Escape!™ © Disney; **174/175** Fireworks at Downtown Disney Pleasure Island, © Disney; **176** Typhoon Lagoon Water Park, © Disney

Every effort has been made to trace the copyright holders, and we apologise in advance for any unintentional omissions or errors. We would be pleased to apply any corrections in any following edition of this publication.

Dear Reader

Your comments, opinions and recommendations are very important to us. Please help us to improve our travel guides by taking a few minutes to complete this simple questionnaire.

You do not need a stamp (unless posted outside the UK). If you do not want to cut this page from your guide, then photocopy it or write your answers on a plain sheet of paper.

Send to: **The Editor, AA World Travel Guides, FREEPOST SCE 4598, Basingstoke RG21 4GY.**

Your recommendations...

We always encourage readers' recommendations for restaurants, nightlife or shopping – if your recommendation is used in the next edition of the guide, we will send you a **FREE AA Guide** of your choice from this series. Please state below the establishment name, location and your reasons for recommending it.

_____
_____
_____
_____
_____

Please send me **AA Guide** _____

About this guide...

Which title did you buy?
  AA _____
Where did you buy it? _____
When? m m / y y
Why did you choose this guide? _____
_____
_____
_____

Did this guide meet your expectations?

Exceeded ☐ Met all ☐ Met most ☐ Fell below ☐

Were there any aspects of this guide that you particularly liked? _____
_____
_____

continued on next page...

Is there anything we could have done better? _____
_____
_____
_____

About you...
Name (*Mr/Mrs/Ms*) _____
Address _____
_____
_____ Postcode _____

Daytime tel nos _____
Email _____

Please only give us your mobile phone number or email if you wish to hear from us about other products and services from the AA and partners by text or mms, or email.

Which age group are you in?
Under 25 ☐   25–34 ☐   35–44 ☐   45–54 ☐   55–64 ☐   65+ ☐

How many trips do you make a year?
Less than one ☐   One ☐   Two ☐   Three or more ☐

Are you an AA member? Yes ☐   No ☐

About your trip...
When did you book? m m / y y   When did you travel? m m / y y

How long did you stay? _____

Was it for business or leisure? _____

Did you buy any other travel guides for your trip? _____

If yes, which ones? _____
_____
_____

Thank you for taking the time to complete this questionnaire. Please send it to us as soon as possible, and remember, you do not need a stamp (*unless posted outside the UK*).

AA Travel Insurance call 0800 072 4168 or visit www.theAA.com

The information we hold about you will be used to provide the products and services requested and for identification, account administration, analysis, and fraud/loss prevention purposes. More details about how that information is used is in our privacy statement, which you'll find under the heading "Personal Information" in our terms and conditions and on our website: www.theAA.com. Copies are also available from us by post, by contacting the Data Protection Manager at AA, Fanum House, Basing View, Basingstoke, Hampshire RG21 4EA.

We may want to contact you about other products and services provided by us, or our partners (by mail, telephone or email) but please tick the box if you DO NOT wish to hear about such products and services from us by mail, telephone or email. ☐